Micropython STM32 Program

First Edition
Sarful Hassan

Preface

Welcome to the MicroPython STM32 Programming Guide, designed to simplify and enhance your journey in programming STM32 microcontrollers using MicroPython. This book bridges the gap between Python's simplicity and the powerful STM32 development ecosystem, making it suitable for beginners and professionals alike. MicroPython offers an intuitive way to work with hardware, allowing developers to prototype faster, learn embedded systems concepts easily, and reduce development complexity. This book focuses on the STM32 NUCLEO-F446RE, providing hands-on guidance, practical examples, and structured learning.

Whether you're a hobbyist, a student, or an experienced engineer, this guide equips you with the knowledge and tools to master MicroPython programming on STM32 boards.

Who This Book Is For

This book is intended for:

- Hobbyists eager to explore hardware programming without the steep learning curve of traditional C/C++.
- Students in engineering programs who wish to learn MicroPython as an introductory language for embedded systems.
- Professionals, such as embedded engineers, looking for a quick prototyping tool to complement traditional development workflows.
- Educators seeking a structured resource to introduce embedded programming concepts.

No prior experience with STM32 or MicroPython is required, but familiarity with Python basics will be helpful.

How This Book Is Organized

This book is divided into multiple sections to guide you from basic concepts to advanced programming.

1. Introduction to MicroPython provides an overview of MicroPython and its relevance to embedded systems.
2. Getting to Know STM32 NUCLEO-F446RE gives detailed insights into the hardware and features of the STM32 board.
3. Setting Up the Development Environment offers step-by-step instructions for installing tools and flashing MicroPython firmware.

4. Programming Basics covers syntax, data types, and control structures.
5. Hardware Interfacing explores digital I/O, analog I/O, and advanced communication protocols.
6. Advanced Topics discusses bitwise operations, random number generation, and compound operators for efficient programming.

Each chapter is accompanied by practical examples and exercises to help you apply the concepts learned.

What Was Left Out

To maintain focus and clarity, the following topics are not covered in this book:

- Deep Dive into STM32 HAL Libraries: The book focuses on MicroPython instead of STM32 HAL or LL libraries.
- Advanced RTOS Concepts: Topics like FreeRTOS and multi-threading are not included.
- Comprehensive Circuit Design: While hardware usage is explained, detailed PCB design or electrical schematics are beyond the scope of this book.

Code Style (About the Code)

This book adheres to Python's PEP 8 standards for code readability and consistency. All examples are indented with four spaces, written with clear and descriptive variable names, and designed for practical use on the STM32 NUCLEO-F446RE. Readers are encouraged to experiment with the code and adapt it to their projects.

Release Notes

This is the First Edition of the MicroPython STM32 Programming Guide. Future editions may include expanded support for other STM32 boards, topics on integration with cloud platforms for IoT, and additional chapters on advanced debugging and optimization.

Notes on the First Edition

The first edition emphasizes clarity and practical application. It has been peer-reviewed by experts in MicroPython and STM32 development to ensure accuracy and relevance. Suggestions for improvement are welcome at mechatronicslab@gmail.com.

MechatronicsLAB Online Learning

For additional learning resources, tutorials, and project ideas, visit:
Website: mechatronicslab.net
Email Support: mechatronicslab@gmail.com
Join our community of developers and enthusiasts to share knowledge and collaborate on exciting projects.

How to Contact Us

For inquiries, feedback, or technical support, contact us at:
Email: mechatronicslab@gmail.com
Website: mechatronicslab.net
We value your input and are committed to enhancing your learning experience.

Acknowledgments for the First Edition

We extend our gratitude to our readers for inspiring us to create this guide, contributors including engineers, developers, and educators who reviewed and enriched the content, and the MechatronicsLAB Team for their dedication to fostering education in embedded systems. Special thanks to the STM32 Community and the creators of MicroPython for making this possible.

Table of Contents

Introduction to MicroPython

Chapter Overview

MicroPython is a lean, efficient implementation of Python designed specifically for microcontrollers and embedded systems. It allows developers to write Python code to control hardware, making it accessible and easy to create embedded applications. This chapter introduces the basics of MicroPython, its features, reasons for using it with STM32 microcontrollers, and a step-by-step guide to installing and setting up MicroPython on the STM32 NUCLEO-F446RE board.

Chapter Goal

- Understand the core concepts and features of MicroPython.
- Learn why MicroPython is an excellent choice for STM32 microcontrollers.
- Follow a step-by-step guide to install and set up MicroPython on STM32 NUCLEO-F446RE.

1.1 Overview of MicroPython

MicroPython is a lightweight version of Python 3 optimized to run on microcontrollers and embedded systems. Developed by Damien George in 2014, MicroPython brings the simplicity and readability of Python to embedded programming. It is designed to be efficient and run on limited hardware, enabling developers to work with small devices like STM32 microcontrollers.

MicroPython can execute Python code directly on the microcontroller, providing an interactive environment for real-time development, testing, and debugging. Through the use of MicroPython's REPL (Read-Evaluate-Print Loop) interface, developers can interact with their code directly, making it a powerful tool for both beginners and professionals.

Key Benefits of MicroPython

- **User-Friendly Syntax**: MicroPython retains Python's easy-to-read and easy-to-write syntax, making it accessible for both beginners and experienced programmers.
- **Real-Time Interaction**: MicroPython's REPL allows developers to write, test, and debug code interactively, accelerating the development process.
- **Efficiency**: MicroPython is specifically optimized for small, memory-constrained devices, allowing developers to run Python on microcontrollers with limited resources.
- **Cross-Platform Compatibility**: MicroPython can run on various microcontroller architectures, such as STM32, ESP8266, ESP32, and RP2040, making it versatile for different hardware platforms.

1.2 Key Features of MicroPython

MicroPython includes a range of features that make it ideal for embedded applications. Some of the core features include:

1.2.1 Compact Python 3 Syntax

MicroPython is a minimal subset of Python 3, designed to provide Python's key functionality with a smaller memory footprint. While some advanced Python features are absent to optimize performance, MicroPython still offers a powerful set of tools for embedded systems.

1.2.2 Real-Time REPL (Read-Evaluate-Print Loop)

The REPL interface is an interactive shell where developers can execute Python commands and immediately see results. This allows for real-time testing and debugging of code on the microcontroller, making development faster and more efficient.

1.2.3 Lightweight Standard Libraries

MicroPython includes libraries similar to those in Python's standard library but optimized for embedded systems. These libraries provide functions for handling data types, strings, math operations, file handling, and even common hardware protocols like UART, I2C, and SPI.

1.2.4 GPIO and Hardware Control

MicroPython supports GPIO (General Purpose Input/Output) control, enabling interaction with hardware components such as LEDs, sensors, motors, and displays. It also supports communication protocols like UART, I2C, and SPI, making it ideal for interfacing with various peripherals.

1.2.5 Low-Level Access to Hardware

MicroPython allows direct access to the microcontroller's hardware, enabling control over timers, interrupts, PWM (Pulse Width Modulation), ADC (Analog-to-Digital Conversion), and DAC (Digital-to-Analog Conversion). This level of control is essential for tasks that require precise timing and signal processing.

1.3 Why Use MicroPython with STM32 Microcontrollers

STM32 microcontrollers, particularly the STM32 NUCLEO series, are widely used in embedded systems for their performance, peripheral support, and energy efficiency. The STM32 NUCLEO-F446RE board is an ideal choice for MicroPython due to its compatibility, processing power, and extensive GPIO options.

Key Reasons to Use MicroPython with STM32

1. **Ease of Development and Debugging**
   - MicroPython simplifies the development process with its Python-based syntax and REPL interface. Developers can directly interact with the STM32 board, test code in real time, and troubleshoot issues efficiently.

2. **Powerful STM32 Hardware**
   - The STM32 NUCLEO-F446RE features a 32-bit ARM Cortex-M4 processor, providing excellent performance for a wide range of applications. Combined with MicroPython, this hardware enables the execution of complex code without compromising speed or responsiveness.
3. **Wide Peripheral Support**
   - STM32 microcontrollers support peripherals such as UART, I2C, SPI, and ADC/DAC, making them suitable for sensor data acquisition, motor control, and communication tasks. MicroPython provides access to these peripherals, allowing easy interaction with hardware components.
4. **Flexible and Scalable**
   - STM32 boards offer a scalable solution for embedded applications, from basic projects to more complex systems. Using MicroPython, developers can scale their projects with additional components and advanced functionality without requiring a deep understanding of low-level programming.
5. **Cost-Effective Solution**
   - MicroPython and STM32 NUCLEO boards offer a low-cost solution for embedded systems development. The NUCLEO-F446RE provides powerful capabilities at an affordable price, making it accessible for hobbyists, students, and professionals.

Getting to Know STM32 NUCLEO-F446RE

Chapter Overview

The STM32 NUCLEO-F446RE is a powerful development board featuring the STM32F446RE microcontroller, designed for embedded applications. With a range of peripherals and GPIO pins, it offers flexibility for both basic and advanced projects. In this chapter, we'll provide an overview of the STM32 NUCLEO-F446RE hardware, discuss its specifications, guide you through setting up the board with MicroPython, and introduce STM32CubeMX for configuring and flashing firmware.

Chapter Goal

- Understand the hardware features and specifications of the STM32 NUCLEO-F446RE.
- Learn how to set up the STM32 NUCLEO-F446RE with MicroPython.
- Use STM32CubeMX to configure and flash firmware on the board.

2.1 STM32 NUCLEO-F446RE Hardware Overview

The STM32 NUCLEO-F446RE development board is part of STMicroelectronics' NUCLEO series, designed to provide a flexible platform for developing embedded applications with the STM32 microcontroller family. It is equipped with the STM32F446RE microcontroller, which is based on an ARM Cortex-M4 core, and has a wide variety of I/O pins and interfaces for diverse application needs.

Key Features of the STM32 NUCLEO-F446RE

- **Microcontroller**: STM32F446RE, ARM Cortex-M4 core running up to 180 MHz.
- **Flash Memory**: 512 KB Flash memory for code storage.
- **RAM**: 128 KB SRAM, suitable for most embedded applications.
- **Clock Speed**: 180 MHz, providing excellent processing power.
- **Onboard ST-LINK/V2-1 Debugger**: Enables easy debugging, programming, and flashing.
- **Arduino-Compatible Headers**: Allows easy connection with Arduino-compatible shields and modules.
- **Flexible Power Options**: Can be powered via USB or external power sources.
- **Connectivity**: Supports UART, I2C, SPI, CAN, USB, and other communication interfaces.

The STM32 NUCLEO-F446RE provides an excellent balance of performance, flexibility, and ease of use, making it suitable for both beginners and advanced users.

Key Components on the Board

- **Microcontroller (STM32F446RE)**: The main processing unit of the board.
- **ST-LINK/V2-1**: An integrated debugger/programmer, which allows users to program the microcontroller without additional tools.
- **Arduino-Compatible Headers**: Enables easy attachment of Arduino shields, expanding the board's capabilities.
- **User LED and Button**: Includes an onboard LED (LED1) and a user button (B1), which can be used for testing basic I/O functions.
- **Power LED (LD3)**: Indicates that the board is powered and ready for use.

2.2 Microcontroller Specifications and Capabilities

STM32 Nucleo-F401RE Development Board Guid

The STM32 Nucleo-F401RE is a highly versatile development board designed for prototyping with the STM32F401RET6 microcontroller, a member of the ARM Cortex-M4 family. It combines robust performance, power efficiency, and flexibility, making it ideal for embedded systems, IoT, and robotics projects.

- **Key Advantages**:
  - Compatible with Arduino UNO R3 shields.
  - Extended functionality with STM32 Morpho headers.
  - Integrated ST-LINK/V2-1 for seamless debugging and programming.

Key Features

1. **Microcontroller**: STM32F401RET6
   - 32-bit ARM Cortex-M4 processor with a Floating Point Unit (FPU).
   - Operates at a clock speed of 84 MHz.
2. **Memory**:
   - 512 KB Flash Memory for program storage.
   - 96 KB SRAM for efficient data handling.
3. **Power Supply**:
   - Operates at 3.3V internally.
   - Supports external input voltage of 7V-12V via VIN.
   - USB-powered with an onboard voltage regulator.
4. **Onboard Debugger**: Integrated ST-LINK/V2-1 supporting SWD and JTAG protocols.
5. **Pin Compatibility**:
   - Arduino UNO R3 headers for shield integration.
   - STM32 Morpho headers for access to all GPIOs and peripherals.
6. **LEDs and Buttons**:
   - **LD1**: USB communication indicator.
   - **LD2**: User-programmable LED.
   - **LD3**: Power indicator.

- o Two Push Buttons: One for reset and another for user control.

Pinout Configuration

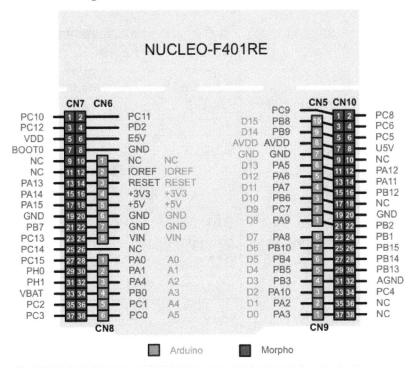

NUCLEO-F401RE

1. Arduino-Compatible Headers

- Provides compatibility with Arduino shields.
- Divided into four categories: CN5, CN6, CN8, CN9.

Category	Pin Type	Pin Names	Description
CN6 (Power)	Reference Voltage	IOREF	3.3V reference voltage pin for shields.
	Reset	RESET	Resets the microcontroller.
	Power Output	+3.3V, +5V	Provides 3.3V and 5V output.

	Ground	GND	System ground pins.
CN8 (Analog)	Analog Input Pins	A0, A1	Analog pins for voltage measurement (12-bit ADC).
	I2C Communication	A4 (SDA), A5 (SCL)	I2C communication pins.
CN5 (Digital)	Digital GPIO Pins	D8-D15	General-purpose digital input/output pins.
	SPI Communication	D10 (CS), D11 (MOSI), D12 (MISO), D13 (SCK)	SPI communication.
CN9 (USART)	Digital GPIO Pins	D0-D7	Digital GPIO pins.
	UART Communication	D0 (Rx), D1 (Tx)	UART/USART communication pins.

2. STM32 Morpho Headers

- Two rows of male headers (CN7 and CN10) provide access to extended GPIOs and peripherals.

Category	Pin Type	Pin Names	Description
CN7	GPIO Pins	PC0-PC3, PC10-PC15, PA0-PA15	General-purpose GPIO pins for peripherals.

	Power	VBAT, +3.3V, +5V, VIN	Power input/output pins.
	Reset	RESET	Resets the microcontroller.
	Reference Voltage	IOREF	3.3V reference voltage.
CN10	GPIO Pins	PA2-PA12, PB1-PB15, PC4-PC9	Additional GPIO pins.
	Power	U5V, GND, AGND	Power and ground pins.

Technical Specifications

Feature	Details
Microcontroller	STM32F401RET6 (ARM Cortex M4)
Architecture	ARM Cortex M4 with Floating Point Unit (FPU)
Clock Speed	84 MHz
Memory	512 KB Flash, 96 KB SRAM
GPIO Pins	50
ADC	12-bit, 16 channels
Timers	16-bit (6), 32-bit (2)
Communication Interfaces	4x USART/UART, 3x I2C, 3x SPI

USB Support	USB 2.0 Full-Speed
RTC	Integrated 32kHz oscillator with calibration
Power Input	7V-15V (VIN), USB-powered
Operating Voltage	1.7V-3.6V (MCU), 3.3V system
Power Consumption	2.4 µA (standby without RTC)
Crystal Oscillators	Internal (16 MHz), External (4-26 MHz)
Onboard Debugger	ST-LINK/V2-1, supports SWD and JTAG

Hardware Details

1. **Microcontroller: STM32F401RET6**
   - High-performance ARM Cortex-M4 core.
   - Supports complex mathematical operations with its Floating Point Unit (FPU).
   - Low power consumption for efficient applications.
2. **Arduino Compatibility**
   - Pinout matches Arduino UNO R3, making it easy to use existing Arduino shields.
   - Simplifies development for users transitioning from Arduino to STM32.
3. **STM32 Morpho Headers**
   - Provides access to all the microcontroller's GPIOs and peripherals.
   - Useful for advanced projects requiring additional functionality.
4. **Integrated Debugger**
   - ST-LINK/V2-1 allows for debugging and programming without external hardware.
   - Supports firmware upgrade for added features.

5. **LEDs and Buttons**
   - LEDs:
     - **LD1**: USB communication activity.
     - **LD2**: Programmable for user-defined functions.
     - **LD3**: Power indication.
   - Buttons:
     - User button for custom input.
     - Reset button for restarting the MCU.

Power Supply Options
- **USB Powered**: Connect via a micro-USB cable for 5V input.
- **VIN Pin**: External power supply (7V-12V recommended, up to 15V).
- **3.3V Pin**: Directly power the MCU using a regulated 3.3V input.
- **Battery Power**: Connect a coin cell battery to VBAT for RTC functionality.

Performance Highlights
- **Speed and Efficiency**: With an 84 MHz clock and advanced peripherals, the STM32 Nucleo-F401RE offers superior performance compared to many 8-bit development boards.
- **Versatility**: Combines Arduino compatibility with advanced STM32 features for a wide range of applications.
- **Debugging Capability**: Built-in ST-LINK debugger supports real-time debugging and step-through code execution.

Setting Up the Development Environment

Chapter Overview

A properly configured development environment is essential for efficient programming, debugging, and testing with MicroPython on the STM32 NUCLEO-F446RE. This chapter covers the required tools, installing and configuring popular MicroPython IDEs (such as Thonny and uPyCraft), setting up serial communication for REPL access, and basic commands for using the REPL to develop and interact with MicroPython code.

Chapter Goal

- Understand the tools and software required for STM32 MicroPython development.
- Install and configure IDEs (Thonny, uPyCraft) for MicroPython development.
- Set up serial communication for MicroPython REPL access.
- Learn essential REPL commands for testing and debugging.

3.1 Required Tools and Software

To set up your development environment for MicroPython on STM32 NUCLEO-F446RE, you'll need a few essential tools and software.

3.1.1 STM32 NUCLEO-F446RE Board

- This is the development board you'll be programming. Ensure it's working properly and can connect to your computer via USB.

3.1.2 USB Cable (Type-A to Micro-B)

- Used to connect the STM32 NUCLEO board to your computer for power, programming, and serial communication.

3.1.3 MicroPython Firmware

- The MicroPython firmware for STM32 is available on the official MicroPython website and must be flashed onto the STM32 NUCLEO board. Ensure you have downloaded and installed it as described in the previous chapter.

3.1.4 Integrated Development Environment (IDE)

- Using an IDE makes it easier to write, upload, and debug MicroPython code. We recommend either **Thonny** or **uPyCraft** for MicroPython development, both of which are simple and user-friendly.

3.1.5 STM32CubeProgrammer

- This tool allows you to flash MicroPython firmware onto the STM32 NUCLEO board. It's available for download from the STMicroelectronics website.

3.1.6 Serial Communication Software (Optional)

- If you need additional control or troubleshooting, a serial terminal such as **PuTTY** or **Tera Term** can be useful. These tools enable you to connect to the REPL without an IDE.

3.2 Installing and Configuring MicroPython IDEs

Several IDEs support MicroPython, but Thonny and uPyCraft are among the most popular for their simplicity and ease of use. In this section, we'll cover how to install and configure both.

3.2.1 Thonny IDE

Thonny is a beginner-friendly Python IDE with built-in support for MicroPython, making it ideal for working with STM32 and other microcontrollers.

Steps to Install Thonny

1. **Download Thonny**: Visit https://thonny.org and download the installer for your operating system (Windows, macOS, or Linux).
2. **Install Thonny**: Run the downloaded installer and follow the prompts to install Thonny on your computer.

Configuring Thonny for MicroPython

1. **Launch Thonny**: Open the Thonny application after installation.
2. **Set the Interpreter**:
   - Go to **Tools > Options**.
   - In the **Interpreter** tab, select **MicroPython (Generic)** from the drop-down list.
3. **Connect to the STM32 NUCLEO Board**:
   - Connect the STM32 NUCLEO-F446RE board to your computer via USB.
   - Under **Port**, select the COM port associated with your STM32 board (e.g., COM3 on Windows or /dev/ttyUSB0 on Linux).
4. **Confirm Connection**:
   - Click **OK** to save the settings.
   - In the Thonny editor, you should see a REPL (Read-Evaluate-Print Loop) prompt. If you see >>>, you're connected and ready to start programming.

Writing and Running a Simple Script

In Thonny, type a simple script such as:

```
print("Hello from STM32!")
```

1. Click **Run** or press F5 to execute the code. The output should display in the REPL.

3.2.2 uPyCraft IDE

uPyCraft is a lightweight IDE designed specifically for MicroPython and provides easy access to REPL and file management for MicroPython devices.

Steps to Install uPyCraft

1. **Download uPyCraft**: You can find the installer for uPyCraft on DFRobot's website.
2. **Install uPyCraft**: Run the installer and follow the prompts to install the IDE on your system.

Configuring uPyCraft for MicroPython

1. **Launch uPyCraft**: Open the uPyCraft application after installation.
2. **Select the COM Port**:
   ○ Connect your STM32 NUCLEO-F446RE board to your computer.
   ○ Go to **Tools > Serial** and select the COM port corresponding to your STM32 board.
3. **Set the Board Type**:
   ○ Go to **Tools > Board** and choose **STM32F4** (or similar compatible option if STM32 NUCLEO-F446RE is not listed).
4. **Connect to the Board**:
   ○ Click on the **Connect** button in the toolbar. If the connection is successful, the REPL should appear, showing the >>> prompt.

Writing and Running a Simple Script

In the editor window, write a basic script, for example:

```
print("Hello from uPyCraft on STM32!")
```

1. Click **Download and Run** to execute the code on your STM32 board. The output will appear in the REPL.

3.3 Serial Communication Setup for MicroPython REPL

The REPL (Read-Evaluate-Print Loop) provides an interactive way to test and execute commands in MicroPython. You can access the REPL via serial communication if you prefer not to use an IDE or need direct access for troubleshooting.

3.3.1 Using a Serial Terminal (e.g., PuTTY, Tera Term)

Steps to Set Up a Serial Terminal

1. **Download and Install a Terminal Program**: Options include PuTTY (Windows) and Tera Term (Windows and Linux).
2. **Connect the STM32 Board**: Ensure the STM32 NUCLEO-F446RE is connected to your computer via USB.
3. **Open the Terminal Program**:
   - In **PuTTY**: Open PuTTY, select **Serial** as the connection type, and set the COM port and baud rate.
   - In **Tera Term**: Open Tera Term, select **Serial**, choose the correct COM port, and set the baud rate.
4. **Configure the Serial Settings**:
   - Baud rate: **115200**
   - Data bits: **8**
   - Parity: **None**
   - Stop bits: **1**
   - Flow control: **None**
5. **Access the REPL**: Once connected, you should see the >>> prompt, indicating that REPL is ready. You can now enter commands directly into the REPL.

3.4 Basic Commands and Using REPL for Development

The REPL interface allows you to interact with MicroPython in real-time. In this section, we'll cover basic REPL commands and examples to help you get comfortable with the interactive environment.

3.4.1 REPL Basics

- **>>>**: The REPL prompt, where you type commands and press Enter to execute.
- **Real-Time Feedback**: Any output from executed commands appears immediately in the REPL, making it an excellent tool for testing and debugging.

3.4.2 Basic REPL Commands

1. **Printing Output**
   - Command: `print("Hello, World!")`
   - Description: Displays text or variable values in the REPL. Useful for debugging.

Example:
```
>>> print("Hello, STM32!")

Hello, STM32!
```

2. **Assigning Variables**
   - Command: `variable_name = value`
   - Description: Assigns a value to a variable, storing it in memory.

Example:
```
>>> x = 10
>>> print(x)
10
```

3. **Mathematical Operations**
   - o Command: `result = expression`
   - o Description: Performs arithmetic operations like addition, subtraction, multiplication, and division.

Example:

```
>>> result = 5 + 3
>>> print(result)
8
```

4. **Control GPIO Pins**

Command:

```
from machine import Pin
led = Pin(13, Pin.OUT)
led.value(1)  # Turn LED on
led.value(0)  # Turn LED off
```

   - o Description: Controls GPIO pins directly from the REPL, which is useful for hardware testing.

Example:
```
>>> from machine import Pin
>>> led = Pin(13, Pin.OUT)
>>> led.value(1)  # Turns the onboard LED on
```

5. **Accessing Help**
   - o Command: `help()`
   - o Description: Displays help information about MicroPython commands and functions.

Example:

```
>>> help()
```

6. **Importing Modules**
   - Command: `import module_name`
   - Description: Imports MicroPython modules to access functions and classes.

Example:

```
>>> import time
>>> time.sleep(1)  # Pauses execution for 1 second
```

3.4.3 Using REPL for Debugging

- **Testing Code in Small Segments**: Use REPL to test individual lines or functions.
- **Real-Time Output**: Print statements provide instant feedback for tracking variables and program flow.
- **Error Handling**: REPL displays error messages immediately, helping to quickly identify and fix issues.

Basic MicroPython Syntax

Chapter Overview

MicroPython is a streamlined version of Python designed specifically for embedded systems. While it retains the core syntax and structure of Python, MicroPython has a few differences to make it compatible with hardware constraints. This chapter covers the basic syntax of MicroPython, compares it to standard Python, and provides examples for writing and running a simple MicroPython program.

Chapter Goal

- Understand the similarities and differences between MicroPython and standard Python.
- Learn the basic syntax used in MicroPython.
- Write and execute a simple MicroPython program on the STM32 NUCLEO-F446RE.

4.1 MicroPython vs. Python: Similarities and Differences

MicroPython is based on Python 3, so it shares many similarities in syntax, data types, and programming constructs. However, due to memory and processing limitations on microcontrollers, some features of Python are either modified or omitted in MicroPython.

4.1.1 Similarities between MicroPython and Python

MicroPython retains most of Python's core features, making it familiar for Python developers. Here are the main similarities:

1. **Basic Syntax and Structure**:
   - MicroPython uses Python's indentation-based structure for code blocks.
   - It supports Python's basic constructs, such as `if`, `for`, `while`, and `def` for defining functions.

2. **Data Types**:
   - MicroPython supports Python's basic data types, including integers, floats, strings, lists, tuples, and dictionaries.
3. **Control Flow Statements**:
   - `if`, `else`, and `elif` statements function the same way in MicroPython.
   - Loops (`for` and `while`) also work similarly.
4. **Functions and Modules**:
   - You can define functions with `def` and import modules with `import`, just like in Python.
   - Many standard modules like `math`, `time`, and `random` are available in MicroPython.
5. **Exception Handling**:
   - MicroPython includes Python's `try`, `except`, and `finally` blocks for handling errors.

4.1.2 Differences between MicroPython and Python

Despite the similarities, MicroPython has a few limitations compared to standard Python:

1. **Limited Libraries**:
   - MicroPython has a subset of the Python standard library. Some libraries, especially those requiring large memory (like `pandas`, `numpy`, or `scipy`), are not available.
2. **No __main__ Module**:
   - Unlike standard Python, MicroPython scripts do not have a `__main__` block. The script starts execution from the top.
3. **Hardware-Specific Modules**:
   - MicroPython includes modules for hardware control, such as `machine` for GPIO, I2C, SPI, and ADC/DAC operations. These modules are not available in standard Python.

4. **Memory Management**:
   - MicroPython has limited memory, so some Python features (like complex data structures and large libraries) may not work efficiently.
5. **Differences in `time` Module**:
   - The `time` module in MicroPython is simplified, with only basic functions like `sleep()`, `sleep_ms()`, and `sleep_us()` for delays.
6. **File Handling**:
   - File handling in MicroPython is supported but is limited to basic operations (especially on microcontrollers without an onboard filesystem).

Summary of Key Differences

Feature	Python	MicroPython
Standard Library	Extensive, includes libraries like `os` and `pandas`	Limited, includes a subset for embedded use
Hardware Control	Not available	Uses modules like `machine` for GPIO control
Memory Management	Larger capacity	Limited memory and stack size
File Handling	Full support, including open and file modes	Basic support, varies by board
`time` Module	Full suite of functions	Simplified for embedded systems

4.2 Writing and Running a Simple MicroPython Program

Writing and running code in MicroPython is straightforward, especially for users familiar with Python. In this section, we'll write a simple MicroPython program, then run it on the STM32 NUCLEO-F446RE to demonstrate basic functionality.

4.2.1 Writing a Simple Program

To start with MicroPython, let's create a basic program that:

- Prints a welcome message.
- Performs a basic calculation.
- Controls the onboard LED (if available).

Example Code: Simple Program

Here's a simple MicroPython program:

```python
# Simple MicroPython Program

# Print a welcome message
print("Welcome to MicroPython on STM32!")

# Perform a basic calculation
a = 5
b = 3
result = a + b
print("The result of", a, "+", b, "is:", result)

# Control the onboard LED (if available)
from machine import Pin
import time

# Define the LED pin (pin number may vary by board)
led = Pin(13, Pin.OUT)

# Blink the LED 5 times
for i in range(5):
    led.on()                # Turn LED on
    print("LED is ON")
    time.sleep(1)           # Delay for 1 second
    led.off()               # Turn LED off
    print("LED is OFF")
    time.sleep(1)
```

This program does three things:

1. Prints a welcome message to the console.
2. Adds two numbers and displays the result.
3. Blinks an LED five times using a `for` loop.

4.2.2 Understanding the Code

Printing a Welcome Message

The `print()` function outputs a message to the console, just like in Python. This can be useful for debugging or providing user feedback.

```
print("Welcome to MicroPython on STM32!")
```

Performing a Basic Calculation

Variables a and b are assigned integer values, and a calculation (a + b) is performed. The result is stored in `result` and printed.

```
a = 5
b = 3
result = a + b
print("The result of", a, "+", b, "is:", result)
```

Controlling the Onboard LED

The onboard LED is accessed using the `machine.Pin` module. By toggling the LED on and off with a delay, we can create a blinking effect.

```
from machine import Pin
import time

led = Pin(13, Pin.OUT)   # Define the LED pin

for i in range(5):
    led.on()             # Turn LED on
    time.sleep(1)        # Wait for 1 second
    led.off()            # Turn LED off
    time.sleep(1)
```

4.2.3 Running the Program

To run this MicroPython program on your STM32 NUCLEO-F446RE, follow these steps:

Step 1: Open Thonny or uPyCraft IDE

1. **Connect the STM32 Board**: Ensure your STM32 NUCLEO-F446RE is connected to your computer.
2. **Open the IDE**: Launch either Thonny or uPyCraft.
3. **Select the MicroPython Interpreter**: Set the interpreter to MicroPython (Generic).

Step 2: Write the Code

- Copy the example code into a new file in the IDE.

Step 3: Save and Run the Code

1. **Save the Code**: Save the file with a `.py` extension (e.g., `blink_led.py`).
2. **Run the Code**:
   - In Thonny, press **Run** or press F5 to execute the script.
   - In uPyCraft, select **Download and Run**.

Expected Output

- The welcome message and calculation result should print to the console.
- The LED on the STM32 board should blink five times, with messages indicating when the LED is on and off.

Troubleshooting Tips

- **Check the LED Pin**: If the onboard LED does not blink, double-check the pin number. Some STM32 boards may have a different pin assignment for the LED.
- **Verify Connection**: Ensure the STM32 NUCLEO board is properly connected to the computer and that the IDE recognizes it.

Digital I/O in STM32

Chapter Overview

Digital I/O (Input/Output) is a fundamental aspect of embedded systems, enabling a microcontroller to interact with the physical world by controlling LEDs, reading button presses, and interfacing with other digital devices. Using MicroPython on the STM32 NUCLEO-F446RE allows you to configure GPIO (General Purpose Input/Output) pins easily for digital operations. This chapter covers how to set up and use digital I/O pins for input and output and includes a practical project.

Chapter Goal

- Learn how to configure GPIO pins as digital input and output on STM32 NUCLEO-F446RE.
- Use MicroPython to control outputs (e.g., turning an LED on and off).
- Read digital input from devices like buttons and use the input to control other outputs.

Rules

- **Initialize GPIO Pins Correctly**: Set each GPIO pin as input or output based on its use.
- **Use Pull-Up or Pull-Down Resistors for Inputs**: Stabilize input readings by configuring internal pull-up or pull-down resistors.
- **Control Outputs with on( ) and off( )**: These methods simplify setting outputs high or low.
- **Debounce Button Inputs**: For stable readings, use a delay to debounce button presses.
- **Optimize Code for Performance**: Avoid unnecessary loops and delays to maximize efficiency.

Syntax Table

Serial No	Topic	Code Snippet	Simple Example
1	Configure GPIO as Output	`pin = Pin(pin_number, Pin.OUT)`	`led = Pin("A1", Pin.OUT)`
2	Configure GPIO as Input	`pin = Pin(pin_number, Pin.IN, Pin.PULL_UP)`	`button = Pin("A2", Pin.IN, Pin.PULL_UP)`
3	Set Output High	`pin.on()`	`led.on()`
4	Set Output Low	`pin.off()`	`led.off()`
5	Toggle Output State	`pin.value(not pin.value())`	`led.value(not led.value())`
6	Read Digital Input	`value = pin.value()`	`button_state = button.value()`
7	Delay	`time.sleep(seconds)`	`time.sleep(0.1)`

Topic Explanations

1. Configure GPIO as Output

What is Configuring GPIO as Output?

Configuring a GPIO pin as an output allows the STM32 NUCLEO-F446RE to control external devices, such as LEDs or relays, by setting the pin to high or low.

Use Purpose

- **Control Digital Devices**: Activates or deactivates LEDs, motors, or other components.
- **Provide High or Low Signals**: Outputs binary signals that drive external devices.

Syntax

```
pin = Pin(pin_number, Pin.OUT)
```

Syntax Explanation

- **Pin**: MicroPython class for GPIO control.
- **pin_number**: The specific pin identifier, such as "A1".
- **Pin.OUT**: Configures the pin as an output, enabling it to drive external devices.
- **Pin Class**: Allows MicroPython to manage GPIO functionality on the specified pin.
- **Pin.OUT Mode**: Sets the pin to output mode, making it capable of outputting high or low signals.

Simple Code Example

```
from machine import Pin
led = Pin("A1", Pin.OUT)   # Configures pin A1 as an output for LED
```

Code Example Explanation

- **Configures A1 as Output**: The pin is set as an output, allowing control over the LED connected to it.

Notes

- Ensure the correct pin is used based on your board's pin layout.
- Output pins should not exceed the current limit of the microcontroller.

Warnings

- Exceeding the current rating may damage the microcontroller.

---

2. Configure GPIO as Input

What is Configuring GPIO as Input?

Configuring a GPIO pin as an input allows the STM32 to read digital states from devices, such as buttons or sensors, providing a high or low signal to indicate an active or inactive state.

Use Purpose

- **Read Button Presses**: Detects if a button is pressed.
- **Monitor Digital Sensors**: Reads binary signals from external sensors.

Syntax

```
pin = Pin(pin_number, Pin.IN, Pin.PULL_UP)
```

Syntax Explanation

- **Pin**: MicroPython GPIO class.
- **pin_number**: The specific pin to configure as input (e.g., "A2").
- **Pin.IN**: Configures the pin as an input to read incoming signals.
- **Pin.PULL_UP / Pin.PULL_DOWN**: Internal resistors to stabilize the input state by defaulting it to high or low.
- **Pull-Up/Down Resistors**: Useful for preventing floating inputs that can lead to unreliable readings.
- **Input Mode**: Configures the pin for reading digital input signals.

Simple Code Example

```
from machine import Pin
button = Pin("A2", Pin.IN, Pin.PULL_UP)  # Configures pin A2 as input
with pull-up
```

Code Example Explanation

- **Configures A2 with Pull-Up**: Allows reading a button connected to the pin, with the pull-up resistor ensuring stable readings.

Notes

- Pull-up is common for buttons, which often connect to ground when pressed.
- Without a pull-up/down, the input may float, causing unstable readings.

Warnings

- Floating inputs can produce unreliable results; always use pull resistors.

---

3. Set Output High

What is Setting Output High?

Setting a digital output pin to high (1) activates the connected component, such as turning an LED on. The pin outputs a voltage level (usually 3.3V or 5V).

Use Purpose

- **Turn On LEDs or Other Components**: Sends a high signal to connected devices.
- **Control Digital Outputs**: Provides a high output to drive the device.

Syntax

```
pin.on()
```

Syntax Explanation

- **pin**: The output pin.
- **on()**: Method that sets the pin to a high (1) state, sending voltage to the connected device.
- **High State**: Provides power to the component, equivalent to setting pin.value(1).

Simple Code Example

```
led.on()  # Sets the LED to high (on)
```

Code Example Explanation

- **Turns on the LED**: The LED connected to led is set to high, powering the LED.

Notes

- Use on() instead of manually setting pin.value(1) for clarity.

Warnings

- Exceeding current limits for the pin may damage the microcontroller.

---

4. Set Output Low

What is Setting Output Low?

Setting an output pin to low (0) deactivates the connected component, such as turning an LED off by pulling the pin to ground.

Use Purpose

- **Turn Off LEDs or Other Components**: Sends a low signal to deactivate the device.
- **Control Digital Outputs**: Provides a low output to control the device.

Syntax

```
pin.off()
```

Syntax Explanation

- **pin**: The output pin.
- **off()**: Method that sets the pin's state to low (0), grounding the connected component.
- **Low State**: Equivalent to pin.value(0), turning off the component.

Simple Code Example

```
led.off()  # Sets the LED to low (off)
```

Code Example Explanation

- **Turns off the LED**: Sets the pin low, turning off the LED.

Notes

- Use off() for clarity over pin.value(0).

Warnings

- Ensure setting the pin low does not conflict with the circuit.

---

5. Toggle Output State

What is Toggling Output State?

Toggling an output pin switches its state between high and low, allowing for operations like blinking an LED.

Use Purpose

- **Blink LEDs**: Alternates the state to create a blink pattern.
- **Switch State of Outputs**: Useful for toggling outputs on and off.

Syntax

```
pin.value(not pin.value())
```

Syntax Explanation

- **pin**: The output pin.
- **value()**: Method to get or set the pin's current state.
- **not**: Logical operator that inverts the current state.
- **Toggle Logic**: Alternates the output state each time the code executes.

Simple Code Example

```
led.value(not led.value())  # Toggles LED state
```

Code Example Explanation

- **Alternates the LED state**: Each call will turn the LED on if it's off, and off if it's on.

Notes

- Toggle in loops for periodic on/off actions.
- Ideal for LEDs or indicator lights.

---

6. Read Digital Input

What is Reading Digital Input?

Reading a digital input pin retrieves its current state, either high (1) or low (0), allowing the STM32 to detect conditions like button presses.

Use Purpose

- **Monitor Button State**: Checks if a button is pressed.
- **Read Digital Sensors**: Reads binary data from external sensors.

Syntax

```
value = pin.value()
```

Syntax Explanation

- **value**: Variable to store the pin's state (0 or 1).
- **pin**: The input pin to read.
- **value()**: Method that returns the current state, either high (1) or low (0).
- **Return Value**: High if the input is active, low if inactive.

Simple Code Example

```
button_state = button.value()  # Reads the button state
```

Code Example Explanation

- **Stores the button state**: button_state is 1 if the button is not pressed (high) and 0 if pressed (active-low).

Notes

- Use pull-up/pull-down resistors for stable readings.

- Useful in loops to monitor digital inputs.

Warnings
- Unconnected inputs can float; always use pull resistors.

Final Project: LED Control with Button Input

Project Name

Button-Controlled LED Toggle

Project Objective

Use a button input to toggle an LED on and off with each press.

Project Circuit

Component	STM32 Pin	Connection Details
Button	A2	Connect one side to GND and the other to A2 with pull-up
LED with Resistor	A1	Connect LED to A1 with a resistor, other end to GND

Project Code

```python
from machine import Pin
import time

# Configure LED pin as output
led = Pin("A1", Pin.OUT)

# Configure button pin as input with pull-up resistor
button = Pin("A2", Pin.IN, Pin.PULL_UP)

while True:
    if button.value() == 0:  # Check if button is pressed (active-low)
        led.value(not led.value())  # Toggle LED state
        time.sleep(0.2)  # Debounce delay
```

Save and Run

1. Save the code as main.py on your STM32 NUCLEO.

2. Run the script; pressing the button toggles the LED's state.

Check Output

The LED should toggle on and off with each button press, demonstrating how to control digital inputs and outputs on the STM32 NUCLEO-F446RE using MicroPython.

Analog I/O in STM32

Chapter Overview

Analog I/O (Input/Output) allows the STM32 to interact with real-world, continuous signals. This is particularly useful for reading variable signals from sensors (e.g., temperature or light sensors) and controlling outputs (e.g., LED brightness or motor speed) with precision. In the STM32 NUCLEO-F446RE, analog inputs are read using ADC (Analog-to-Digital Converter), while analog-like outputs are generated using PWM (Pulse Width Modulation).

Chapter Goal

- Learn to configure ADC for reading analog inputs.
- Use PWM to control the intensity of outputs.
- Implement a project to control an LED's brightness with a potentiometer, using ADC and PWM in MicroPython.

Rules

- **Select the Correct ADC Pin**: ADC-compatible pins on the STM32 NUCLEO are limited, so ensure you're using a compatible pin (e.g., "A1" for ADC).
- **Adjust PWM Frequency for Different Devices**: LEDs, motors, and servos respond differently to PWM; choose an appropriate frequency.
- **Use Proper Conversion and Scaling**: ADC readings range from 0 to 4095 (12-bit resolution); PWM duty cycles use 0 to 65535.

- **Averaging for Stability**: Reducing noise is essential when reading from sensors; average multiple samples for smoother data.
- **Avoid Rapid Sampling**: Introducing delays between ADC reads improves accuracy by reducing noise.

Syntax Table

Serial No	Topic	Code Snippet	Simple Example
1	Configure ADC (Analog Input)	`adc = ADC(Pin(pin_number))`	`sensor = ADC(Pin("A1"))`
2	Read ADC Value	`value = adc.read_u16()`	`sensor_value = sensor.read_u16()`
3	Configure PWM Output	`pwm = PWM(Pin(pin_number), freq=freq)`	`led_pwm = PWM(Pin("A2"), freq=1000)`
4	Set PWM Duty Cycle	`pwm.duty_u16(value)`	`led_pwm.duty_u16(32768)`
5	Set PWM Frequency	`pwm.freq(freq)`	`led_pwm.freq(2000)`
6	Delay	`time.sleep(seconds)`	`time.sleep(0.1)`

Topic Explanations

1. Configure ADC (Analog Input)

What is Configuring ADC for Analog Input?

The ADC (Analog-to-Digital Converter) enables the STM32 to interpret varying analog voltages by converting them into a digital value. With MicroPython, ADC configuration allows reading of analog signals, typically with a range of 0V to 3.3V, and converting them to a digital value between 0 and 4095 (for 12-bit resolution).

Use Purpose

- **Read Sensor Data**: Convert sensor readings (e.g., temperature, light) to digital values.
- **Analyze Voltage Levels**: Allows the STM32 to measure varying signals in real-time.

Syntax

```
adc = ADC(Pin(pin_number))
```

Syntax Explanation

- **ADC**: A MicroPython class that enables analog-to-digital conversion on the specified pin.
- **Pin**: Specifies the pin number for ADC.
- **pin_number**: Identifier for the analog input pin, like "A1" for the STM32 NUCLEO-F446RE.
- **ADC Object**: Configures the pin to receive analog signals, allowing analog data to be read as digital values.
- **Pin Class**: Ensures the correct configuration of the pin to support analog input.

Simple Code Example

```
from machine import ADC, Pin
sensor = ADC(Pin("A1"))  # Configures pin A1 for analog input
```

Code Example Explanation

- **Configures A1 as ADC Input**: Sets A1 as an analog input, preparing it to receive and interpret signals from an analog sensor.

Notes

- The ADC range is typically 0–4095 for 12-bit resolution.
- Analog voltage range is limited to 0–3.3V; inputs higher than 3.3V could damage the microcontroller.

Warnings

- Ensure the connected device outputs a voltage within the safe range (0–3.3V) for the STM32.

2. Read ADC Value

What is Reading an ADC Value?

Reading an ADC value provides a digital representation of the analog voltage on the pin. For STM32 NUCLEO-F446RE, the ADC is usually 12-bit, so the read value ranges from 0 (0V) to 4095 (3.3V).

Use Purpose

- **Capture Analog Signal Strength**: Measure the strength of analog signals.
- **Interpret Sensor Data**: Convert analog signals to quantifiable digital values for sensors.

Syntax

```
value = adc.read_u16()
```

Syntax Explanation

- **value**: Stores the digital value of the analog reading.
- **adc**: The ADC object created for the analog input pin.
- **read_u16()**: Reads the analog value as a 16-bit integer (0–65535) for higher precision.
- **Precision**: Although the STM32's ADC is 12-bit (0–4095), read_u16() outputs a 16-bit value to allow for more granular scaling.
- **Scaling**: This 16-bit representation (0–65535) can be scaled down to interpret 12-bit values more precisely.

Simple Code Example

```
sensor_value = sensor.read_u16()  # Reads analog value from sensor
```

Code Example Explanation

- **Reads ADC Value**: sensor_value contains the current analog reading as a digital value.

Notes

- To convert the 16-bit ADC value to voltage: (sensor_value / 65535) * 3.3.
- Averaging multiple readings can help reduce noise.

3. Configure PWM Output

What is Configuring PWM Output?

Pulse Width Modulation (PWM) is a technique that allows a digital output pin to simulate analog output by rapidly toggling between high and low states. PWM outputs are used to control components requiring varying power, such as LEDs and motors, by adjusting the duty cycle.

Use Purpose

- **Control Brightness and Speed**: Adjusts LED brightness or motor speed by changing the duty cycle.
- **Simulate Analog Output**: Mimics analog signals with variable duty cycles on a digital pin.

Syntax

```
pwm = PWM(Pin(pin_number), freq=freq)
```

Syntax Explanation

- **PWM**: MicroPython class for setting up PWM on a GPIO pin.
- **Pin**: Specifies the GPIO pin for PWM output.
- **pin_number**: Identifier for the PWM-capable pin, such as "A2".
- **freq**: Frequency in Hertz (Hz), setting the PWM toggle rate.
- **PWM Frequency**: Frequency defines how often the PWM signal completes a cycle; different frequencies are better suited for different applications (e.g., 1 kHz for LEDs, 20 kHz for motors).
- **Pin Class**: Configures the specified pin for PWM output.

Simple Code Example

```
from machine import PWM, Pin
led_pwm = PWM(Pin("A2"), freq=1000)   # Configures pin A2 for PWM output
at 1 kHz
```

Code Example Explanation
- **Sets Up PWM at 1kHz on A2**: The `led_pwm` object can now control brightness on an LED connected to A2 by varying the duty cycle.

Notes
- Choose the frequency based on your application: higher frequencies for smooth motor control, lower frequencies for visible LED effects.
- Experiment with different frequencies for optimal results in your application.

Warnings
- Using extremely high frequencies can cause overheating and power loss.

---

4. Set PWM Duty Cycle

What is Setting PWM Duty Cycle?
The duty cycle determines the percentage of time the PWM signal stays high in each cycle. A higher duty cycle results in a higher average output voltage, making LEDs appear brighter or motors run faster.

Use Purpose
- **Adjust LED Brightness or Motor Speed**: Controls the intensity of the device connected to the pin.
- **Simulate Analog Output Control**: Provides finer control over digital devices.

Syntax
```
pwm.duty_u16(value)
```

Syntax Explanation
- **pwm**: The PWM object initialized for output.
- **duty_u16()**: Method to set the PWM duty cycle.

- **value**: A 16-bit value (0–65535) representing the duty cycle, where 0 is 0% and 65535 is 100%.
- **Duty Cycle Value**: Higher values result in longer "on" times per cycle, creating a brighter or faster effect.
- **16-Bit Range**: Allows precise duty cycle adjustments, suitable for sensitive applications like smooth dimming.

Simple Code Example

```
led_pwm.duty_u16(32768)   # Sets duty cycle to 50% for half brightness
```

Code Example Explanation
- **Sets Duty Cycle to 50%**: Provides half brightness for an LED by setting the duty cycle to 50%.

Notes
- Use values like 16384 for 25%, 32768 for 50%, and 49152 for 75% brightness.
- Duty cycles closer to 0 or 65535 give dim or full brightness, respectively.

Warnings
- High duty cycles can cause heating in LEDs and motors; use proper current-limiting resistors.

5. Set PWM Frequency

What is Setting PWM Frequency?
PWM frequency controls how fast the output toggles between high and low states. Different applications benefit from different frequencies for smooth and efficient control.

Use Purpose
- **Prevent Visible LED Flicker**: Higher frequencies prevent noticeable flickering.
- **Optimize Control of Motors**: Smoothes motor response for quieter, more efficient operation.

Syntax

```
pwm.freq(freq)
```

Syntax Explanation

- **pwm**: The PWM object.
- **freq**: Desired frequency in Hertz (Hz), setting the number of cycles per second.
- **Frequency Range**: Low frequencies (100 Hz) for visual effects, high frequencies (2 kHz and above) for motors.
- **Impact on Devices**: Higher frequencies create smoother analog effects, ideal for sensitive applications.

Simple Code Example

```
led_pwm.freq(500)   # Sets PWM frequency to 500 Hz
```

Code Example Explanation

- **Sets Frequency to 500Hz**: The LED will blink at a rate that prevents visible flickering.

Notes

- PWM frequency impacts power efficiency: lower frequencies conserve power for LEDs, higher frequencies for motors.
- Experiment with different frequencies for best results with your hardware.

Warnings

- Very high frequencies can increase current consumption and cause overheating.

Final Project: Control LED Brightness with a Potentiometer

Project Objective

Use an ADC input to read the potentiometer value and adjust the brightness of an LED using PWM based on this input.

Project Circuit

Component	STM32 Pin	Connection Details
Potentiometer	A1	Connect one end to 3.3V, the other to GND, and wiper to A1
LED with Resistor	A2	Connect LED to A2 through a resistor, with the other end to GND

Project Code

```python
from machine import ADC, Pin, PWM
import time

# Configure the potentiometer on ADC pin A1
pot = ADC(Pin("A1"))

# Configure the LED for PWM output on A2
led_pwm = PWM(Pin("A2"), freq=1000)

while True:
    # Read potentiometer value (0-65535)
    pot_value = pot.read_u16()

    # Set LED brightness based on potentiometer reading
    led_pwm.duty_u16(pot_value)

    # Delay for stable reading
    time.sleep(0.1)
```

Save and Run

1. Save this code as main.py on your STM32 NUCLEO.
2. Run the script; rotating the potentiometer will adjust the LED's brightness accordingly.

Check Output

The LED brightness should increase or decrease as you turn the potentiometer, demonstrating the ADC and PWM features on STM32.

Advanced I/O in STM32

Chapter Overview

Advanced I/O allows embedded systems to interact with a variety of peripherals and external components. By using advanced I/O techniques, such as interrupts, UART, I2C, and SPI, STM32 NUCLEO-F446RE can communicate effectively with sensors, displays, and other microcontrollers. This chapter covers configuring and using these interfaces with MicroPython.

Chapter Goal

- Understand how to configure and use interrupts for responsive input handling.
- Learn to set up UART, I2C, and SPI communication for connecting with external peripherals.
- Implement a project that uses UART to transmit and receive data between STM32 and a computer.

Rules

- **Use Interrupts for Immediate Response**: Avoid using polling in time-critical applications; use interrupts for efficient event-driven programming.
- **Set Correct Baud Rates for UART**: Ensure matching baud rates between devices for reliable communication.
- **Address I2C Devices Correctly**: Use the correct I2C addresses for each device on the I2C bus to avoid conflicts.
- **Match SPI Settings**: Configure SPI mode, clock polarity, and phase to match the peripheral requirements.
- **Optimize Code for Each Communication Protocol**: Understand the unique characteristics of each protocol (UART, I2C, SPI) for optimal implementation.

Syntax Table

Serial No	Topic	Code Snippet	Simple Example
1	Configure GPIO with Interrupt	`pin = Pin(pin_number, Pin.IN, Pin.PULL_UP)`	`button = Pin("A1", Pin.IN, Pin.PULL_UP)`
2	Set Interrupt Callback	`pin.irq(trigger=Pin.IRQ_FALLING, handler=callback)`	`button.irq(trigger=Pin.IRQ_FALLING, handler=callback)`
3	Configure UART	`uart = UART(uart_number, baudrate=baud_rate)`	`uart = UART(2, baudrate=9600)`
4	Send UART Data	`uart.write(data)`	`uart.write("Hello")`
5	Read UART Data	`data = uart.read()`	`received_data = uart.read()`
6	Configure I2C	`i2c = I2C(i2c_number, scl=Pin(scl_pin),`	`i2c = I2C(1, scl=Pin("B8"), sda=Pin("B9"))`

		sda=Pin(sda_pi n))	
7	Scan I2C Bus	devices = i2c.scan()	devices = i2c.scan()
8	Send I2C Data	i2c.writeto(ad dress, data)	i2c.writeto(0x40, b'\x01')
9	Read I2C Data	data = i2c.readfrom(a ddress, nbytes)	data = i2c.readfrom(0x40, 2)
10	Configure SPI	spi = SPI(spi_number , baudrate=baud_ rate, polarity=polar ity, phase=phase)	spi = SPI(1, baudrate=500000)
11	Send SPI Data	spi.write(data)	spi.write(b'\x01\x 02')
12	Read SPI Data	data = spi.read(nbyte s)	data = spi.read(2)

Topic Explanations

1. Configure GPIO with Interrupt

What is Configuring GPIO with Interrupt?

Interrupts allow the STM32 to respond immediately to changes in GPIO input, such as button presses. By setting a GPIO pin with an interrupt, the microcontroller can pause normal execution to respond to the event, and then resume normal operation.

Use Purpose

- **Immediate Event Detection**: Detects button presses, sensor triggers, or other input changes in real-time.
- **Avoid Polling**: Reduces the need for constantly checking the pin state, saving processing power.

Syntax

```
pin = Pin(pin_number, Pin.IN, Pin.PULL_UP)
pin.irq(trigger=Pin.IRQ_FALLING, handler=callback)
```

Syntax Explanation

- **Pin**: The GPIO class used to configure the pin as an input.
- **pin_number**: Identifier for the GPIO pin, such as "A1".
- **Pin.IN**: Sets the pin as an input.
- **Pin.PULL_UP**: Adds a pull-up resistor to stabilize the input.
- **irq()**: Method to configure an interrupt on the pin.
- **trigger**: Specifies when the interrupt should activate, such as Pin.IRQ_FALLING (on a low signal).
- **handler**: Function to call when the interrupt triggers.

Simple Code Example

```python
from machine import Pin
import time

# Configure pin A1 as input with pull-up resistor
button = Pin("A1", Pin.IN, Pin.PULL_UP)

# Define the interrupt handler function
def callback(pin):
    print("Button pressed")

# Set up an interrupt on the button pin
button.irq(trigger=Pin.IRQ_FALLING, handler=callback)
```

Code Example Explanation

- **Sets Up Button with Interrupt**: The button triggers the `callback` function whenever it is pressed.

Notes

- Debouncing may still be necessary to avoid multiple triggers for a single press.
- `Pin.IRQ_RISING` is used for detecting a high signal.

Warnings

- Avoid using delays within interrupt handlers, as it can lead to timing issues.

---

2. Configure UART

What is Configuring UART?

UART (Universal Asynchronous Receiver/Transmitter) is a communication protocol for serial data exchange between the STM32 and other devices, such as computers, GPS modules, or Bluetooth modules. UART is commonly used for sending and receiving data in text format.

Use Purpose

- **Communicate with Other Devices**: Sends data to and receives data from peripherals.
- **Debugging and Monitoring**: Transfers data between the STM32 and a serial monitor on a computer.

Syntax

```
uart = UART(uart_number, baudrate=baud_rate)
```

Syntax Explanation

- **UART**: MicroPython class for configuring UART communication.
- **uart_number**: UART interface number on the STM32 (usually 1, 2, or 3).

- **baudrate**: Communication speed in bits per second, such as 9600 or 115200.

Simple Code Example

```
from machine import UART
uart = UART(2, baudrate=9600)   # Set up UART2 with 9600 baud rate
```

Code Example Explanation

- **Configures UART with 9600 Baud Rate**: Prepares UART2 for communication at a standard baud rate, allowing data to be transmitted or received.

Notes

- Ensure matching baud rates between devices for reliable communication.
- UART can be used to send and receive data continuously in a loop.

Warnings

- Use uart.read() carefully to avoid buffer overflow.

---

3. Configure I2C

What is Configuring I2C?

I2C (Inter-Integrated Circuit) is a protocol used for communication between multiple devices over two wires: SDA (data) and SCL (clock). Each device has a unique address on the bus, allowing multiple devices to communicate with the STM32.

Use Purpose

- **Connect Multiple Peripherals**: Interfaces with devices like sensors, displays, and EEPROMs.
- **Communicate Using Addressing**: Each device has a unique address for selective communication.

Syntax

```
i2c = I2C(i2c_number, scl=Pin(scl_pin), sda=Pin(sda_pin))
```

Syntax Explanation

- **I2C**: MicroPython class for configuring I2C communication.
- **i2c_number**: Specifies the I2C interface number.

- **scl**: Defines the clock line (SCL) pin.
- **sda**: Defines the data line (SDA) pin.

Simple Code Example

```
from machine import I2C, Pin
i2c = I2C(1, scl=Pin("B8"), sda=Pin("B9"))  # Set up I2C1 with B8 (SCL)
and B9 (SDA)
```

Code Example Explanation

- **Sets Up I2C with SCL on B8 and SDA on B9**: Configures I2C1 for communication with external devices.

Notes

- Use `i2c.scan()` to detect devices and get their addresses.
- Devices on the I2C bus must have unique addresses.

Warnings

- Incorrect pin connections can cause communication failure.

---

4. Configure SPI

What is Configuring SPI?

SPI (Serial Peripheral Interface) is a synchronous protocol for high-speed communication between devices. It uses three lines (MOSI, MISO, SCK) and often a fourth line (CS) for chip select, enabling communication with one device at a time on the bus.

Use Purpose

- **High-Speed Communication**: Interfaces with devices like displays, memory chips, and sensors requiring fast data transfer.
- **Allows Multiple Devices**: Uses chip select (CS) to communicate with multiple peripherals.

Syntax

```
spi = SPI(spi_number, baudrate=baud_rate, polarity=polarity,
phase=phase)
```

Syntax Explanation

- **SPI**: MicroPython class for configuring SPI communication.
- **spi_number**: Specifies the SPI interface number.

- **baudrate**: Communication speed.
- **polarity**: Sets the idle state of the clock line.
- **phase**: Determines the clock phase for data capture.

Simple Code Example

```
from machine import SPI, Pin
spi = SPI(1, baudrate=500000)  # Set up SPI1 with 500 kHz baud rate
```

Code Example Explanation

- **Configures SPI1 with 500 kHz Baud Rate**: Prepares SPI1 for high-speed data transfer.

Notes

- Configure polarity and phase to match device requirements.
- Use separate CS lines for each SPI device.

Warnings

- Incorrect settings for polarity and phase may lead to corrupted data.

Final Project: UART Communication Between STM32 and a Computer

Project Objective

Set up UART communication between the STM32 NUCLEO-F446RE and a computer to send and receive text data, using the serial monitor on the computer.

Project Code

```
from machine import UART
import time

# Set up UART2 at 9600 baud rate
uart = UART(2, baudrate=9600)

while True:
    # Check if data is available to read
    if uart.any():
        received_data = uart.read()
        print("Received:", received_data)

        # Send a response back to the computer
        uart.write("Data received: " + received_data.decode('utf-8') +
"\n")

    # Delay to avoid excessive processing
    time.sleep(0.1)
```

Save and Run

1. Save this code as `main.py` on your STM32 NUCLEO.
2. Open a serial monitor on the computer, set to the matching baud rate (9600), and connect to the correct COM port.
3. Type messages in the serial monitor to send data to the STM32 and observe responses.

Check Output

The STM32 should display received data on the serial monitor and respond with "Data received: [your message]." This demonstrates bidirectional UART communication.

Time Functions in STM32

Chapter Overview

Time functions are essential in embedded systems for controlling timing, delays, and event scheduling. STM32's MicroPython provides easy-to-use time functions, allowing you to create delays, measure elapsed time, and manage real-time events using the Real-Time Clock (RTC). This chapter covers how to use these time functions with the STM32 NUCLEO-F446RE.

Chapter Goal

- Learn to create delays and measure elapsed time with MicroPython.
- Understand the Real-Time Clock (RTC) and its setup in STM32.
- Implement a project to display elapsed time and real-time clock data on a serial monitor.

Rules

- **Use Delays Appropriately**: Avoid excessive delays in real-time applications where responsiveness is crucial.
- **Use Time Measurement for Precise Control**: Measure elapsed time for tasks like benchmarking and event scheduling.
- **Set RTC Correctly**: Configure the RTC with the correct date and time to ensure accurate timekeeping.
- **Avoid Blocking Code**: Consider non-blocking alternatives for time-sensitive applications instead of traditional delays.

Syntax Table

Serial No	Topic	Code Snippet	Simple Example
1	Delay	`time.sleep(seconds)`	`time.sleep(1)`
2	Millisecond Delay	`time.sleep_ms(ms)`	`time.sleep_ms(500)`
3	Microsecond Delay	`time.sleep_us(us)`	`time.sleep_us(1000)`
4	Measure Elapsed Time	`start = time.ticks_ms()`	`start = time.ticks_ms(); elapsed = time.ticks_diff(time.ticks_ms(), start)`
5	Get Current Time in Milliseconds	`time.ticks_ms()`	`current_ms = time.ticks_ms()`
6	Get Current Time in Microseconds	`time.ticks_us()`	`current_us = time.ticks_us()`
7	Initialize RTC	`rtc = RTC()`	`rtc = RTC()`

Topic Explanations

1. Delay

What is Delay?

A delay pauses the execution of the program for a specified time. It's a simple way to control the timing of tasks, such as blinking an LED or waiting for an event.

Use Purpose

- **Control Task Timing**: Delays are commonly used in loops for timing control, like creating a blinking LED effect.
- **Prevent Rapid Execution**: Delays reduce CPU load by slowing down the execution of specific tasks.

Syntax

```
time.sleep(seconds)
```

Syntax Explanation

- **time**: The MicroPython module for time-related functions.
- **sleep()**: Function that pauses program execution.
- **seconds**: The number of seconds to delay, specified as a floating-point value for sub-second delays.

Simple Code Example

```
import time
time.sleep(1)  # Pauses the program for 1 second
```

Code Example Explanation

- **1-Second Delay**: Pauses execution for exactly one second.

Notes

- Delays can be fractional, such as `time.sleep(0.5)` for a half-second delay.
- Avoid long delays in time-sensitive applications.

Warnings

- Excessive delays can block other tasks and make the program unresponsive.

2. Millisecond Delay

What is Millisecond Delay?

A millisecond delay pauses the program for a specified number of milliseconds. This provides finer control over timing in applications where a one-second delay is too long.

Use Purpose

- **Precise Timing Control**: Useful for creating short, precise delays.
- **Control LED Blinking**: Ideal for creating fast blink effects or timing events with millisecond precision.

Syntax

```
time.sleep_ms(ms)
```

Syntax Explanation

- **sleep_ms()**: Function that pauses program execution in milliseconds.
- **ms**: Integer specifying the number of milliseconds to delay.

Simple Code Example

```
import time
time.sleep_ms(500)  # Pauses the program for 500 milliseconds (0.5 seconds)
```

Code Example Explanation

- **500 ms Delay**: Pauses execution for half a second.

Notes

- Use sleep_ms for delays under a second to optimize code readability.
- Can be used in place of sleep() for higher precision in timing.

Warnings

- Frequent millisecond delays can still block other tasks in loops.

3. Microsecond Delay

What is Microsecond Delay?

A microsecond delay pauses the program for a specified number of microseconds. This is used for extremely precise timing, typically in high-speed applications like signal generation.

Use Purpose

- **High-Precision Timing**: Useful for precise control over timing-sensitive tasks.
- **Signal Generation**: Ideal for bit-banging protocols or generating waveforms.

Syntax

```
time.sleep_us(us)
```

Syntax Explanation

- **sleep_us()**: Function that pauses program execution in microseconds.
- **us**: Integer specifying the number of microseconds to delay.

Simple Code Example

```
import time
time.sleep_us(1000)  # Pauses the program for 1000 microseconds (1
millisecond)
```

Code Example Explanation

- **1 ms Delay in Microseconds**: Provides a 1-millisecond delay with microsecond precision.

Notes

- Use only when necessary, as microsecond delays consume significant processing power.
- Ideal for precise timing applications, but avoid in non-critical code.

Warnings

- High-frequency delays can reduce CPU efficiency for other tasks.

4. Measure Elapsed Time

What is Measuring Elapsed Time?

Measuring elapsed time involves recording the current time, performing a task, and then calculating the time taken. This helps monitor the duration of operations and tasks in real-time.

Use Purpose

- **Benchmarking**: Measures the execution time of code sections.
- **Interval Monitoring**: Keeps track of the elapsed time for timed events.

Syntax

```
start = time.ticks_ms()
elapsed = time.ticks_diff(time.ticks_ms(), start)
```

Syntax Explanation

- **ticks_ms()**: Function that returns the current time in milliseconds since the program started.
- **ticks_diff()**: Calculates the difference between two timestamps, providing elapsed time.
- **start**: Timestamp marking the start of an event.

Simple Code Example

```
import time
start = time.ticks_ms()
# Perform a task
elapsed = time.ticks_diff(time.ticks_ms(), start)
print("Elapsed time:", elapsed, "ms")
```

Code Example Explanation

- **Measures Task Duration**: Calculates and displays the time taken to perform a task in milliseconds.

Notes

- Use `ticks_us()` for microsecond precision.
- Useful in performance-critical applications to ensure optimal timing.

5. Initialize RTC

What is RTC Initialization?

The Real-Time Clock (RTC) is a hardware clock that keeps track of date and time. Initializing the RTC on the STM32 allows accurate timekeeping, even when the microcontroller is in low-power modes.

Use Purpose

- **Time and Date Management**: Keeps track of real-world time and date.
- **Event Scheduling**: Useful for applications that need to log data with timestamps.

Syntax

```
rtc = RTC()
```

Syntax Explanation

- **RTC**: MicroPython class for configuring the Real-Time Clock.
- **rtc**: The object created for handling RTC operations.

Simple Code Example

```
from machine import RTC
rtc = RTC()  # Initialize RTC
```

Code Example Explanation

- **Initializes the RTC**: Prepares the RTC module for setting and reading date and time.

Notes

- The RTC can retain time even if the STM32 enters a low-power state.
- Requires accurate time setting for reliable use.

Warnings

- Resetting the STM32 without battery backup may reset the RTC.

6. Set RTC Date and Time

What is Setting RTC Date and Time?

Setting the RTC's date and time allows accurate timekeeping on the STM32. Once set, the RTC can provide current date and time values whenever needed.

Use Purpose

- **Time-Sensitive Applications**: Logs data with timestamps or schedules events.
- **Real-Time Clock Control**: Allows setting and retrieval of the current time and date.

Syntax

```
rtc.datetime((year, month, day, weekday, hour, minute, second,
subseconds))
```

Syntax Explanation

- **datetime()**: Method for setting the RTC date and time.
- **year, month, day, weekday**: Date components.
- **hour, minute, second, subseconds**: Time components.

Simple Code Example

```
rtc.datetime((2024, 11, 10, 1, 15, 30, 45, 0))  # Set date and time
```

Code Example Explanation

- **Sets RTC Date and Time**: Configures the RTC with a specific date and time, allowing for precise real-time tracking.

Notes

- weekday is an integer (0–6) representing Monday to Sunday.
- Set the RTC once, then retrieve the time as needed.

7. Read RTC Date and Time

What is Reading RTC Date and Time?

Reading the RTC provides the current date and time, which is useful for logging, scheduling, and displaying real-time information.

Use Purpose

- **Retrieve Current Time**: Get the exact date and time.
- **Log Timestamps**: Records when events occur for data logging applications.

Syntax

```
current_time = rtc.datetime()
```

Syntax Explanation

- **rtc**: The RTC object.
- **datetime()**: Method to read the current RTC date and time, returning a tuple with date and time components.

Simple Code Example

```
current_time = rtc.datetime()
print("Current Time:", current_time)
```

Code Example Explanation

- **Displays Current Date and Time**: Prints the real-time date and time maintained by the RTC.

Notes

- Returns a tuple with values: (year, month, day, weekday, hour, minute, second, subseconds).
- Useful in applications requiring real-time data logging.

Warnings

- Ensure RTC is initialized and set correctly before reading.

Final Project: Elapsed Time and RTC Display

Project Objective

Create a timer to measure elapsed time and display both elapsed and real-time clock data on the serial monitor.

Project Code

```python
from machine import RTC
import time

# Initialize RTC
rtc = RTC()
rtc.datetime((2024, 11, 10, 1, 15, 30, 0, 0))  # Set date and time

# Record start time
start = time.ticks_ms()

while True:
    # Calculate elapsed time in seconds
    elapsed_ms = time.ticks_diff(time.ticks_ms(), start)
    elapsed_s = elapsed_ms / 1000

    # Get current RTC time
    current_time = rtc.datetime()

    # Display elapsed time and RTC time
    print("Elapsed Time:", elapsed_s, "seconds")
    print("RTC Date and Time:", current_time)

    # Delay 1 second before updating
    time.sleep(1)
```

Save and Run

1. Save the code as main.py on your STM32 NUCLEO.
2. Run the script, and open a serial monitor on your computer to view the elapsed time and current RTC time.

Check Output

The serial monitor should display elapsed time in seconds and update the RTC time every second, demonstrating the use of the RTC and time-based functions on the STM32.

Constants and Variables

Chapter Overview

Constants and variables are foundational elements in programming, allowing the STM32 to store and manipulate data dynamically. Constants represent values that remain fixed throughout the program, while variables hold data that can change as the program executes. This chapter covers defining, initializing, and using constants and variables effectively with MicroPython on the STM32 NUCLEO-F446RE.

Chapter Goal

- Learn how to declare constants and variables in MicroPython.
- Understand when and why to use constants versus variables.
- Use constants and variables in a practical project to control an LED's brightness based on potentiometer input.

Rules

- **Use Uppercase for Constants**: Write constants in uppercase letters to distinguish them from variables.
- **Initialize Variables Before Use**: Avoid errors by always assigning an initial value to variables before using them.
- **Choose Descriptive Names**: Use meaningful names for constants and variables to improve code readability.
- **Use Constants for Fixed Values**: Replace hardcoded values with constants for easier maintenance and understanding.
- **Update Variables as Needed**: Variables can change as the program executes, while constants should remain fixed.

Syntax Table

Serial No	Topic	Code Snippet	Simple Example
1	Define a Constant	`CONSTANT_NAME = value`	`PI = 3.14159`
2	Declare a Variable	`variable_name = value`	`counter = 0`
3	Reassign a Variable	`variable_name = new_value`	`counter = 5`
4	Define Multiple Variables	`var1, var2 = value1, value2`	`x, y = 10, 20`
5	Global Variable Declaration	`global variable_name within a function`	`global counter`
6	Local Variable Declaration	`variable_name inside a function`	`def func(): local_var = 5`
7	Increment a Variable	`variable_name += increment_value`	`counter += 1`

Topic Explanations

1. Define a Constant

What is a Constant?

A constant is a fixed value that doesn't change throughout the program. Constants are useful for storing values that are referenced multiple times and should remain consistent, such as configuration settings or mathematical constants.

Use Purpose

- **Define Unchanging Values**: Constants improve code clarity by representing fixed values that don't need to be reassigned.
- **Avoid Magic Numbers**: Replace hardcoded values with named constants to make code easier to read and maintain.

Syntax

```
CONSTANT_NAME = value
```

Syntax Explanation

- **CONSTANT_NAME**: Name of the constant, typically in uppercase letters to indicate it is fixed. Use meaningful names that describe the purpose of the constant.
  - Examples: `PI`, `MAX_SPEED`, `LED_BRIGHTNESS_LIMIT`.
- **= (Assignment Operator)**: Used to assign a fixed value to the constant.
- **value**: The unchanging data assigned to the constant. This value can be of any data type, such as integers, floats, strings, or lists.
- **Uppercase Convention**: Constants are typically written in uppercase to signal that they are not meant to change.
- **Descriptive Names**: Choose names that clearly indicate the constant's purpose in the code, making it easy for other programmers to understand its use.

Simple Code Example

```
PI = 3.14159  # Define the mathematical constant pi
```

Code Example Explanation

- **Defines PI as a Constant**: The constant `PI` can be referenced in calculations where pi is needed, ensuring consistency without the risk of accidental changes.

Notes

- Using uppercase names for constants is a programming convention; it's not enforced by MicroPython.
- Constants can store various data types, including lists, dictionaries, and even functions.

2. Declare a Variable

What is Variable Declaration?

Declaring a variable in MicroPython means creating a named reference to store data. Unlike constants, variables can change during the program execution, making them suitable for values that vary over time.

Use Purpose

- **Store Dynamic Data**: Variables hold data that may need to be updated, such as sensor readings, user inputs, or calculation results.
- **Track Program State**: Variables are often used to track counters, flags, or status information.

Syntax

```
variable_name = value
```

Syntax Explanation

- **variable_name**: The name given to the variable, which should be descriptive of its purpose. Variable names should be written in lowercase or lowercase with underscores.
  - Examples: `counter`, `sensor_value`, `user_name`.
- **= (Assignment Operator)**: Used to assign an initial value to the variable.
- **value**: The initial value assigned to the variable, which can be of any data type (e.g., integers, floats, strings, or lists) and can be modified later.
- **Descriptive Naming**: The variable name should reflect its role or the data it holds, making the code more readable.
- **Initial Value**: Variables should be initialized to a starting value before they are used in the program, as uninitialized variables can cause runtime errors.

Simple Code Example

```
counter = 0   # Initialize a counter variable with a starting value of 0
```

Code Example Explanation

- **Creates a Counter Variable**: The `counter` variable is initialized at 0, ready to be updated as needed within the program.

Notes

- Variable names in Python must start with a letter or underscore and cannot start with a number.
- Variables can store any data type, including lists, dictionaries, and objects.

Warnings

- Avoid using reserved words (e.g., `print`, `for`, `if`) as variable names, as they are reserved for language functions.

---

3. Reassign a Variable

What is Variable Reassignment?

Variable reassignment is updating the value stored in a variable with a new one. Reassigning variables allows the program to store new data dynamically as conditions change.

Use Purpose

- **Update Program State**: Modify values to keep track of changing data, such as a count, position, or user input.
- **Respond to Inputs**: Change variable values based on interactions with the environment or user inputs.

Syntax

```
variable_name = new_value
```

Syntax Explanation

- **variable_name**: Name of the variable to be updated. The name should match an existing variable that has been previously declared.
    - Examples: `counter`, `sensor_value`, `user_name`.
- **= (Assignment Operator)**: Used to assign a new value to the variable.

- **new_value**: The new data or value assigned to the variable, replacing the previous value.
- **Reassignable Values**: Unlike constants, variables can be reassigned with new data as needed, allowing flexibility in programming.
- **Single Line Reassignment**: In MicroPython, reassignment is done directly on a single line without additional syntax.

Simple Code Example

```
counter = 0  # Initial value
counter = 5  # Update counter to a new value
```

Code Example Explanation

- **Updates the Counter**: Changes the value of counter from 0 to 5. The variable can be updated multiple times as needed.

Notes

- Variables can be reassigned any number of times within the program.
- Be careful with reassignments in loops or conditional statements, as it can lead to unexpected results.

---

4. Define Multiple Variables

What is Defining Multiple Variables?

Multiple variable declaration allows initializing multiple variables in a single line, making code more concise and organized. This is especially useful when working with related values that are initialized together.

Use Purpose

- **Simplify Code**: Reduce the number of lines required to declare variables.
- **Group Related Data**: Initialize multiple variables that are logically connected in one statement.

Syntax

```
var1, var2 = value1, value2
```

Syntax Explanation

- **var1, var2**: Names of the variables being initialized. Each name should be descriptive of the variable's purpose.
  - Examples: `x`, `y`, `width`, `height`, `min_val`, `max_val`.
- **= (Assignment Operator)**: Used to assign values to multiple variables simultaneously.
- **value1, value2**: Initial values assigned to each variable. The values can be of any data type and do not need to match in type.
- **Paired Initialization**: The number of variables on the left side of = must match the number of values on the right.
- **Tuple Unpacking**: In Python, this method is also known as tuple unpacking when used with tuples or lists.

Simple Code Example

```
x, y = 10, 20  # Sets x to 10 and y to 20
```

Code Example Explanation

- **Initializes x and y Together**: Creates two variables x and y with the initial values of 10 and 20, respectively.

Notes

- This syntax is also helpful when assigning multiple return values from a function.
- Use descriptive names for each variable to clarify their roles.

Warnings

- Mismatching the number of variables and values will raise a `ValueError` in Python.

Final Project: LED Brightness Control Using Constants and Variables

Create a program that uses constants and variables to control the brightness of an LED based on input from a potentiometer. The LED brightness will change according to the potentiometer's position, with the brightness capped by a constant.

Project Circuit

Component	STM32 Pin	Connection Details
Potentiometer	A1	Connect one end to 3.3V, the other to GND, and wiper to A1
LED with Resistor	A2	Connect LED to A2 through a resistor, with the other end to GND

Project Code

```python
from machine import ADC, Pin, PWM
import time
# Define constant for maximum brightness
MAX_BRIGHTNESS = 50000
# Initialize potentiometer on ADC pin A1
potentiometer = ADC(Pin("A1"))
# Initialize LED on PWM pin A2
led_pwm = PWM(Pin("A2"), freq=1000)
while True:
    # Read potentiometer value (0-65535)
    sensor_value = potentiometer.read_u16()
    # Calculate brightness as a fraction of MAX_BRIGHTNESS
    brightness = int((sensor_value / 65535) * MAX_BRIGHTNESS)

    # Set LED brightness, capped at MAX_BRIGHTNESS
    led_pwm.duty_u16(brightness)

    # Delay for stability
    time.sleep(0.1)
```

Save and Run

1. Save this code as main.py on your STM32 NUCLEO.
2. Run the script; adjusting the potentiometer will modify the LED's brightness, limited by the MAX_BRIGHTNESS constant.

Check Output

Turning the potentiometer should adjust the LED brightness, with a maximum brightness level set by MAX_BRIGHTNESS.

Data Types in STM32

Chapter Overview

Data types are essential in programming as they define the nature of data stored in variables and how that data can be manipulated. MicroPython on STM32 provides several basic data types, including numbers, strings, lists, tuples, dictionaries, and booleans. Each data type serves specific purposes and supports unique operations. This chapter covers each data type with syntax, examples, and a practical project.

Chapter Goal

- Understand and use different data types in MicroPython.
- Recognize the appropriate data type for various applications.
- Implement a project that demonstrates the use of multiple data types on the STM32.

Rules

- **Choose the Right Data Type for the Task**: Use lists for ordered data, dictionaries for key-value pairs, and tuples for fixed collections.
- **Use Integer and Float for Numeric Operations**: Ensure that calculations are handled with the correct number type.
- **Apply String Methods Carefully**: Strings are immutable; operations return new strings rather than modifying the original.
- **Avoid Mixing Data Types**: Mixing types in operations can lead to unexpected results or errors.
- **Use Boolean for True/False Conditions**: Use booleans for conditions and flags in control flow.

Syntax Table

Serial No	Topic	Code Snippet	Simple Example
1	Integer	`variable_name = 10`	`count = 10`
2	Float	`variable_name = 3.14`	`pi = 3.14159`
3	String	`variable_name = "text"`	`name = "Alice"`
4	List	`variable_name = [item1, item2, item3]`	`numbers = [1, 2, 3, 4]`
5	Tuple	`variable_name = (item1, item2, item3)`	`coordinates = (10, 20)`
6	Dictionary	`variable_name = {key1: value1, key2: value2}`	`student = {"name": "Alice", "age": 20}`
7	Boolean	`variable_name = True or False`	`is_active = True`

Topic Explanations

1. Integer

What is an Integer?

An integer is a whole number without any decimal or fractional part. It can be positive, negative, or zero and is often used in counting, indexing, and arithmetic operations.

Use Purpose

- **Counting and Indexing**: Ideal for tracking counts, indices, or positions.
- **Basic Arithmetic**: Used in calculations that do not require fractions or decimals.

Syntax

```
variable_name = integer_value
```

Syntax Explanation

- **variable_name**: Name of the variable to store the integer.
  - Examples: count, index, num_apples.
- **= (Assignment Operator)**: Used to assign an integer value to the variable.
- **integer_value**: An integer without a decimal, such as 10, -5, or 0.
- **Integer Data Type**: Used for numbers without decimals, ideal for discrete quantities.
- **Assignment**: Assign the integer directly to the variable.

Simple Code Example

```
count = 10  # Initialize count as an integer with value 10
```

Code Example Explanation

- **Creates a Counter**: count holds the integer value 10, which can be used in calculations or loops.

Notes
- Use integers for whole numbers only; switch to float for fractional values.
- Integers support arithmetic operations like addition, subtraction, multiplication, and division.

Warnings
- Dividing integers may convert the result to a float if the result is not a whole number.

---

2. Float

What is a Float?
A float is a number with a decimal point, allowing representation of fractional values. Floats are commonly used in calculations that require precision, such as measurements or percentages.

Use Purpose
- **Precision Calculations**: Used for values that include fractions, such as pi or percentages.
- **Scientific Data**: Ideal for measurements and calculations requiring decimal places.

Syntax
```
variable_name = float_value
```
Syntax Explanation
- **variable_name**: Name of the variable that will hold the float value.
    - Examples: `pi`, `temperature`, `weight`.
- **= (Assignment Operator)**: Assigns a float value to the variable.
- **float_value**: A number with a decimal, such as `3.14`, `-1.5`, or `0.0`.
- **Floating-Point Data Type**: Supports decimal places and fractions for precise values.
- **Decimal Representation**: Floats must include a decimal point (e.g., `3.0` instead of `3`).

Simple Code Example

```
pi = 3.14159  # Assigns the value of pi as a float
```

Code Example Explanation

- **Defines pi as a Float**: The variable pi can be used in calculations needing precise decimal values.

Notes

- Floats are useful for accurate mathematical calculations and scientific data.
- Floats support standard arithmetic operations but may lose precision with very large numbers.

Warnings

- Be cautious of rounding errors in float arithmetic, especially with repeated operations.

---

3. String

What is a String?

A string is a sequence of characters, such as text or alphanumeric data, enclosed in single or double quotes. Strings are often used for names, messages, or any data that includes text.

Use Purpose

- **Store Text Data**: Use strings for names, messages, and identifiers.
- **Display Information**: Ideal for outputting readable information to the user.

Syntax

```
variable_name = "string_value"
```

Syntax Explanation

- **variable_name**: Name of the variable holding the string.
    - Examples: name, message, status.

- **= (Assignment Operator)**: Assigns the string value to the variable.
- **string_value**: Text enclosed in single or double quotes, such as "Hello" or '123'.
- **Text Data Type**: Strings represent text or character sequences.
- **Quotation Marks**: Strings must be enclosed in single (') or double (") quotes.

Simple Code Example

```
name = "Alice"   # Assigns a string with the name Alice
```

Code Example Explanation

- **Stores Name as a String**: The name variable holds the text "Alice" and can be displayed or manipulated as needed.

Notes

- Strings are immutable; methods return new strings instead of modifying the original.
- Common operations include concatenation (+), slicing ([ ]), and length checking (len()).

Warnings

- Strings with both single and double quotes inside require escape characters (e.g., "She said, \"Hello\"").

---

4. List

What is a List?

A list is an ordered collection of elements, which can be of different data types. Lists are mutable, meaning items can be added, removed, or changed.

Use Purpose

- **Store Collections of Data**: Use lists to group related items, such as sensor readings or user inputs.
- **Dynamic Data Structures**: Lists can change size, making them ideal for variable-length data.

Syntax

```
variable_name = [item1, item2, item3]
```

Syntax Explanation

- **variable_name**: Name of the list variable.
  - ○ Examples: numbers, names, temperatures.
- **= (Assignment Operator)**: Assigns a list of items to the variable.
- **[item1, item2, item3]**: List elements enclosed in square brackets, separated by commas. Elements can be any data type.
- **Ordered Collection**: Lists maintain the order of elements as inserted.
- **Mutable Structure**: Elements can be added, removed, or changed in the list.

Simple Code Example

```
numbers = [1, 2, 3, 4]  # List of integers
```

Code Example Explanation

- **Creates a List of Numbers**: numbers holds a sequence of integers, which can be accessed by index.

Notes

- Lists are indexed starting from 0, and negative indices access elements from the end.
- Lists support various methods like append(), remove(), and sort().

Warnings

- Modifying a list while iterating over it can cause errors or unexpected behavior.

5. Tuple

What is a Tuple?

A tuple is similar to a list but is immutable, meaning its elements cannot be changed after creation. Tuples are used for fixed collections of items.

Use Purpose

- **Store Immutable Data**: Use tuples for values that should not be modified.
- **Store Related Items**: Ideal for representing related data, such as coordinates.

Syntax

```
variable_name = (item1, item2, item3)
```

Syntax Explanation

- **variable_name**: Name of the tuple variable.
    - ○ Examples: coordinates, point, dimensions.
- **= (Assignment Operator)**: Assigns the tuple of elements to the variable.
- **(item1, item2, item3)**: Tuple elements enclosed in parentheses, separated by commas.
- **Immutable Structure**: Once defined, the elements of a tuple cannot be changed.
- **Fixed Length**: Tuples have a set length, which can't be altered.

Simple Code Example

```
coordinates = (10, 20)   # Tuple with x and y coordinates
```

Code Example Explanation

- **Defines Coordinates as a Tuple**: coordinates holds fixed values for x and y positions.

Notes

- Tuples are commonly used to group related but unchangeable data.
- Access elements with index syntax, like coordinates[0].

Final Project: Sensor Data Logging with Multiple Data Types

Project Objective

Use various data types to create a program that reads sensor data, logs it with timestamps, and displays it on a serial monitor.

Project Circuit

Component	STM32 Pin	Connection Details
Potentiometer	A1	Connect one end to 3.3V, the other to GND, and wiper to A1

Project Code

```python
from machine import ADC, Pin
import time

# Initialize the potentiometer on ADC pin A1
sensor = ADC(Pin("A1"))

# Constants
NUM_READINGS = 5

# Variables
data_log = []  # List to store readings
count = 0      # Count of readings

while count < NUM_READINGS:
    # Read the sensor value
    reading = sensor.read_u16()

    # Get current timestamp
    timestamp = time.time()

    # Log data as a dictionary with timestamp and reading
    log_entry = {"timestamp": timestamp, "value": reading}

    # Add the entry to the data log
    data_log.append(log_entry)

    # Increment count
    count += 1

    # Print current reading
    print(f"Reading {count}: {log_entry}")
```

```
    # Delay for stability
    time.sleep(1)

# Print all logged data
print("Data Log:", data_log)
```

Save and Run

1. Save this code as main.py on your STM32 NUCLEO.
2. Run the script; it will take five sensor readings and log each one with a timestamp.

Check Output

The program will display each reading and timestamp in the serial monitor, demonstrating the use of integers, lists, dictionaries, and strings.

Data Type Conversion

Chapter Overview

Data type conversion, or casting, is essential in programming, especially in embedded systems, where different data types must be converted to interact effectively. MicroPython on STM32 supports type conversions between integers, floats, strings, booleans, and other types. This chapter covers type conversion techniques in MicroPython, with examples and a practical project that demonstrates data type conversions in an embedded context.

Chapter Goal

- Learn to convert between basic data types, including integers, floats, strings, and booleans.
- Understand when and why to use type conversion to enable seamless data handling.
- Apply type conversion in a practical project that involves sensor data processing and formatting for output.

Rules

- **Convert Data as Needed**: Convert data types based on usage requirements, such as converting integers to strings for display.
- **Use Integer and Float Conversions for Calculations**: Convert values to the appropriate numeric type for mathematical operations.
- **Convert Strings for Display**: Use string conversion when displaying numbers or non-string data.
- **Avoid Unnecessary Conversions**: Only convert data types when necessary to save processing time and memory.
- **Use Boolean Conversion for Conditions**: Convert values to booleans for conditions and control flow.

Syntax Table

Serial No	Topic	Code Snippet	Simple Example
1	Integer Conversion	`int(value)`	`int("10")`
2	Float Conversion	`float(value)`	`float("3.14")`
3	String Conversion	`str(value)`	`str(100)`
4	Boolean Conversion	`bool(value)`	`bool(1)`
5	List to Tuple Conversion	`tuple(list_variable)`	`tuple([1, 2, 3])`
6	Tuple to List Conversion	`list(tuple_variable)`	`list((4, 5, 6))`
7	ASCII Character to Integer	`ord(char)`	`ord("A")`
8	Integer to ASCII Character	`chr(integer)`	`chr(65)`

Topic Explanations

1. Integer Conversion

What is Integer Conversion?

Integer conversion changes a value to an integer type. It's commonly used when you need to perform arithmetic or when a floating-point or string value needs to be treated as a whole number.

Use Purpose

- **Perform Calculations**: Convert values to integers to perform operations like counting, indexing, and other discrete calculations.
- **Remove Decimal Points**: Converting a float to an integer discards the decimal part.

Syntax

```
int(value)
```

Syntax Explanation

- **int()**: The built-in function for converting a value to an integer.
- **value**: The input data to convert, which can be a float, string representing an integer, or boolean.
  - Examples: `"10"`, `3.14`, `True`.
- **String or Float to Integer**: Converts compatible strings or floats by truncating decimal points.
- **Boolean to Integer**: Converts `True` to 1 and `False` to 0.

Simple Code Example

```
number = int("10")  # Converts the string "10" to an integer 10
```

Code Example Explanation

- **Converts String to Integer**: The string `"10"` becomes the integer 10, allowing for arithmetic operations.

Notes

- Invalid strings (e.g., `"ten"`) will cause a `ValueError` when converted to integers.
- Floating-point numbers are truncated to whole numbers (e.g., `int(3.9)` becomes 3).

Warnings

- Converting a float directly may result in a loss of precision due to truncation.

2. Float Conversion

What is Float Conversion?

Float conversion changes a value to a floating-point type, which supports decimal places. This is useful when more precision is needed for calculations.

Use Purpose

- **Precise Calculations**: Converts values to floats to include decimal places in calculations.
- **Convert Numeric Strings to Floats**: Converts compatible strings to floats for arithmetic.

Syntax

```
float(value)
```

Syntax Explanation

- **float()**: The function for converting a value to a float.
- **value**: The input data to convert, which can be an integer or a string representing a float.
  - Examples: "3.14", 100, "0.5".
- **String or Integer to Float**: Allows precision in calculations by representing numbers with decimals.
- **Whole Numbers**: Whole numbers can be converted to floats, resulting in values like 3.0 or 100.0.

Simple Code Example

```
pi_value = float("3.14")  # Converts the string "3.14" to a float
```

Code Example Explanation

- **Converts String to Float**: "3.14" is converted to the float 3.14 for precise arithmetic.

Notes

- Useful for handling measurements, scientific data, or ratios that require decimal points.
- Converting integers results in equivalent floats (e.g., 100 becomes 100.0).

Warnings

- Invalid strings (e.g., "three") will raise a ValueError during conversion.

3. String Conversion

What is String Conversion?

String conversion changes a value to a string, enabling text representation of numbers, booleans, lists, and more.

Use Purpose

- **Display Non-String Data**: Use string conversion to prepare data for display in text format.
- **Combine Text and Numbers**: Convert numbers to strings for concatenation with other text.

Syntax

```
str(value)
```

Syntax Explanation

- **str()**: The built-in function for converting values to strings.
- **value**: The input data to convert, which can be any data type, including integers, floats, booleans, and lists.
  - Examples: 100, 3.14, [1, 2, 3].
- **Non-String to String**: Transforms data into string format for display or storage.
- **Universal Conversion**: Almost all data types can be converted to a string.

Simple Code Example

```
text_value = str(100)  # Converts the integer 100 to the string "100"
```

Code Example Explanation

- **Converts Integer to String**: The integer 100 is now represented as the text "100".

Notes

- Strings are immutable, meaning they cannot be altered directly.
- Commonly used for formatting output and constructing messages.

4. Boolean Conversion

What is Boolean Conversion?

Boolean conversion changes a value to either `True` or `False`. In Python, many values can be converted to booleans, where non-zero numbers and non-empty data are `True`, while zero or empty data are `False`.

Use Purpose

- **Evaluate Conditions**: Boolean conversion is used in control flow, such as `if` statements, to evaluate truthiness.
- **Flagging States**: Convert data to booleans for tracking conditions, such as whether a sensor is active.

Syntax

```
bool(value)
```

Syntax Explanation

- **bool()**: The function for converting a value to a boolean.
- **value**: The input data to convert, which can be any type, including integers, strings, lists, and floats.
    - Examples: 0, `"hello"`, [ ].
- **Non-Zero and Non-Empty to True**: All non-zero numbers, non-empty strings, and non-empty collections are `True`.
- **Zero and Empty to False**: Zero, empty collections, None, and `False` are converted to `False`.

Simple Code Example

```
is_active = bool(1)  # Converts the integer 1 to boolean True
```

Code Example Explanation

- **Converts 1 to True**: The integer 1 is evaluated as `True`, which is useful in conditions.

Notes

- Boolean conversion is essential in conditions and loops.
- Use booleans to simplify conditional expressions and flag states.

Final Project: Sensor Data Processing and Conversion

Project Objective

Create a program that reads data from a sensor, processes the data with type conversions, and displays the data in a readable format.

Project Circuit (In Table)

Component	STM32 Pin	Connection Details
Potentiometer	A1	Connect one end to 3.3V, the other to GND, and wiper to A1

Project Code

```
from machine import ADC, Pin
import time

# Initialize the potentiometer on ADC pin A1
sensor = ADC(Pin("A1"))

# Constants
NUM_READINGS = 5

# Variables
data_log = []   # List to store formatted sensor readings
count = 0       # Counter for readings

while count < NUM_READINGS:
    # Read the sensor value
    raw_value = sensor.read_u16()

    # Convert raw reading to a voltage
    voltage = (raw_value / 65535) * 3.3  # Scale to 3.3V

    # Convert readings to different types for display
    int_value = int(voltage)             # Convert to integer for
display
    text_value = str(voltage)            # Convert to string for logging
    rounded_value = float(f"{voltage:.2f}")  # Round and convert to
float with 2 decimals

    # Log data with formatted values
    log_entry = f"Reading {count + 1}: Voltage={rounded_value}V
(Integer={int_value}, Text='{text_value}')"
    data_log.append(log_entry)
```

```
    # Display the formatted log entry
    print(log_entry)

    # Increment count and delay
    count += 1
    time.sleep(1)

# Display the full data log
print("Data Log:", data_log)
```

Save and Run

1. Save this code as main.py on your STM32 NUCLEO.
2. Run the script; the program will take five sensor readings,
   convert them to different types, and log each one in a
   formatted string.

Check Output

The program will display each sensor reading in various formats on
the serial monitor, demonstrating the use of integer, float, string, and
formatted conversions.

Control Structures in STM32

Chapter Overview

Control structures are essential for making decisions, executing code conditionally, and performing repetitive tasks in programming. In MicroPython on STM32, control structures include conditional statements, loops, and functions, allowing STM32 to make decisions and execute tasks based on certain conditions. This chapter covers the use of control structures with detailed syntax, examples, and a practical project.

Chapter Goal

- Learn to use conditional statements (if, elif, else) to control code execution based on conditions.
- Understand and apply loops (for, while) for repetitive tasks.
- Use functions to organize and reuse code effectively.
- Apply control structures in a practical project on the STM32 to control an LED based on sensor readings.

Rules

- **Use Conditions for Decision-Making**: Use if, elif, and else statements to control program flow based on conditions.
- **Choose the Right Loop Type**: Use for loops for a fixed number of iterations and while loops for condition-based repetition.
- **Define Functions for Reusability**: Functions make code modular and reusable, improving readability.
- **Avoid Excessive Nesting**: Excessive nested loops and conditions reduce code readability.
- **Use break and continue Judiciously**: Use these to control loop behavior, but avoid excessive use for better readability.

Syntax Table

Serial No	Topic	Code Snippet	Simple Example
1	if Statement	if condition:	if temperature > 25:
2	elif Statement	elif condition:	elif temperature == 25:
3	else Statement	else:	else:
4	for Loop	for item in iterable:	for i in range(5):
5	while Loop	while condition:	while sensor_value < 500:
6	break	break	if x > 10: break
7	continue	continue	if x == 0: continue

Topic Explanations

1. if Statement

What is an if Statement?

The if statement is a conditional structure that runs specific code when a given condition is True. If the condition evaluates as True, the code block within the if statement executes; if not, the program skips it.

Use Purpose

- **Make Decisions**: Run code selectively when certain conditions are met.
- **Control Flow**: Directs program flow based on variables or input values.

Syntax

```
if condition:
    # Code to execute if condition is True
```

Syntax Explanation

- **if**: The keyword starting the conditional statement.
- **condition**: An expression that evaluates to True or False.
- **: (Colon)**: Starts the indented block of code.
- **Indented Block**: The code that runs if the condition is True. Proper indentation is required in Python.

Simple Code Example

```
temperature = 30
if temperature > 25:
    print("It's hot!")
```

Code Example Explanation

- **Checks Temperature**: If temperature is greater than 25, it prints "It's hot!"

Notes

- Conditions can include comparison operators (==, !=, >, <) or logical operators (and, or, not).
- Indentation is required for the code within the if block.

Warnings

- Incorrect indentation leads to syntax errors or unintended code execution.

2. `elif` Statement

What is an `elif` Statement?

The `elif` statement checks additional conditions after an initial `if` condition has evaluated as `False`. It allows for multiple conditions to be tested in sequence.

Use Purpose

- **Check Multiple Conditions**: Allows checking multiple conditions in sequence.
- **Provide Alternatives**: Executes different blocks of code depending on conditions.

Syntax

```
if condition1:
    # Code for condition1
elif condition2:
    # Code for condition2
```

Syntax Explanation

- **elif**: Short for "else if," used to add an alternative condition.
- **condition2**: The new condition checked if `condition1` is `False`.
- **Indented Block**: Code to execute if the `elif` condition is `True`.

Simple Code Example

```
temperature = 25
if temperature > 25:
    print("It's hot!")
elif temperature == 25:
    print("It's moderate.")
```

Code Example Explanation

- **Checks Multiple Temperature Ranges**: If `temperature` is 25, it prints "It's moderate."

Notes

- Only one block (`if`, `elif`, or `else`) will execute, even if multiple conditions are `True`.
- Combine `elif` with `if` and `else` to cover all possible cases.

3. `else` Statement

What is an `else` Statement?

The `else` statement provides a default block of code that executes when no preceding `if` or `elif` conditions are met.

Use Purpose

- **Default Action**: Specifies a default action when no conditions are satisfied.
- **Catch-All**: Ensures code execution even if no conditions are True.

Syntax

```
if condition1:
    # Code for condition1
else:
    # Code if no conditions are met
```

Syntax Explanation

- **else**: Begins the default block of code.
- **: (Colon)**: Starts the `else` block.
- **Indented Block**: Code that runs if all other conditions are False.

Simple Code Example

```
temperature = 20
if temperature > 25:
    print("It's hot!")
else:
    print("It's cold.")
```

Code Example Explanation

- **Checks Temperature Range**: If `temperature` is not greater than 25, it defaults to printing "It's cold."

Notes

- The `else` block is optional and should be used when a default action is required.
- Only one `else` block is allowed per `if` statement.

4. for Loop

What is a for Loop?

A for loop iterates over items in a sequence, such as a list, tuple, or range, and executes code for each item.

Use Purpose

- **Iterate Over Sequences**: Perform actions on each item in a collection.
- **Fixed Iterations**: Use for tasks with a predetermined number of repetitions.

Syntax

```
for item in iterable:
    # Code to execute for each item
```

Syntax Explanation

- **for**: Starts the loop.
- **item**: Represents each item in the sequence during each iteration.
- **in**: Keyword specifying the sequence to iterate over.
- **iterable**: A sequence, like a list or range, to loop through.

Simple Code Example

```
for i in range(5):
    print("Iteration:", i)
```

Code Example Explanation

- **Loops 5 Times**: Prints "Iteration: 0", "Iteration: 1", ..., "Iteration: 4".

Notes

- range(n) generates numbers from 0 to n-1.
- Commonly used for iterating over lists, tuples, and other sequences.

5. while Loop

What is a while Loop?

A while loop executes code as long as a specified condition remains True. This loop is useful when the number of iterations is not predetermined.

Use Purpose

- **Conditional Repetition**: Repeat actions until a condition changes.
- **Dynamic Loops**: Ideal for loops that depend on changing conditions.

Syntax

```
while condition:
    # Code to execute while condition is True
```

Syntax Explanation

- **while**: Starts the loop.
- **condition**: Expression controlling the loop; if True, the loop continues.
- **Indented Block**: Code to execute as long as the condition is True.

Simple Code Example

```
counter = 0
while counter < 5:
    print("Counter:", counter)
    counter += 1
```

Code Example Explanation

- **Counts to 4**: The loop runs until counter reaches 5.

Notes

- Ensure that the loop condition eventually becomes False to prevent infinite loops.
- break can be used to exit a while loop early.

6. break

What is break?

The break statement immediately exits the loop, regardless of the loop condition. It is often used to terminate loops early based on a specific condition.

Use Purpose

- **Exit Loop Prematurely**: Allows ending a loop when a condition is met.
- **Optimize Loops**: Avoid unnecessary iterations once a goal is achieved.

Syntax

```
for item in iterable:
    if condition:
        break
```

Syntax Explanation

- **for/while loop**: break can be used in both for and while loops.
- **condition**: Specifies when to break out of the loop.
- **break**: Ends the loop immediately when the condition is met.

Simple Code Example

```
for i in range(10):
    if i == 5:
        break
    print(i)
```

Code Example Explanation

- **Stops at 5**: The loop prints numbers 0 to 4 and exits when i reaches 5.

Notes

- break is useful for finding results quickly within loops.
- It improves loop efficiency by exiting when no further iterations are necessary.

7. continue

What is continue?

The continue statement skips the rest of the code in the current loop iteration and moves to the next iteration, bypassing the remaining code in the loop body.

Use Purpose

- **Skip Specific Iterations**: Use continue to avoid certain cases within a loop.
- **Control Loop Flow**: Bypasses specific actions under certain conditions.

Syntax

```
for item in iterable:
    if condition:
        continue
    # Code to execute if condition is False
```

Syntax Explanation

- **for/while loop**: continue can be used in both for and while loops.
- **condition**: Specifies when to skip the current iteration.
- **continue**: Moves to the next iteration without executing the remaining loop code.

Simple Code Example

```
for i in range(5):
    if i == 2:
        continue
    print(i)
```

Code Example Explanation

- **Skips 2**: The loop prints numbers 0, 1, 3, and 4, skipping 2.

Notes

- continue allows control over specific cases in loops.
- Useful for handling exceptions without stopping the loop entirely.

Final Project: Sensor-Controlled LED Using Control Structures

Project Objective

Create a program that reads a potentiometer and adjusts an LED's brightness based on sensor values. The program uses conditionals to check sensor readings and loops to create an interactive control system.

Project Circuit

Component	STM32 Pin	Connection Details
Potentiomet er	A1	Connect one end to 3.3V, the other to GND, and wiper to A1
LED with Resistor	A2	Connect LED to A2 with a resistor, and the other end to GND

Project Code

```python
from machine import ADC, Pin, PWM
import time

# Initialize potentiometer on ADC pin A1
potentiometer = ADC(Pin("A1"))

# Initialize LED on PWM pin A2
led_pwm = PWM(Pin("A2"), freq=1000)

# Function to calculate brightness based on sensor value
def calculate_brightness(sensor_value):
    if sensor_value < 10000:
        return 0
    elif sensor_value < 30000:
        return int(sensor_value * 0.5)  # Medium brightness
    else:
        return min(sensor_value, 65535)  # Full brightness, capped at
max

while True:
    # Read sensor value
    sensor_value = potentiometer.read_u16()
```

```
# Calculate brightness using a function
brightness = calculate_brightness(sensor_value)

# Set LED brightness
led_pwm.duty_u16(brightness)

# Display sensor value and brightness level
print(f"Sensor Value: {sensor_value}, LED Brightness:
{brightness}")

# Delay for stability
time.sleep(0.1)
```

Save and Run

1. Save this code as main.py on your STM32 NUCLEO.
2. Run the script; rotating the potentiometer will adjust the LED's brightness based on the sensor reading.

Check Output

The LED brightness should increase or decrease as you adjust the potentiometer, with brightness levels determined by conditions in the calculate_brightness function.

Arithmetic Operators in STM32

Chapter Overview

Arithmetic operators perform basic mathematical operations like addition, subtraction, multiplication, and division. These operators are essential for embedded programming, where calculations are often necessary for sensor data processing, signal generation, and controlling hardware outputs. This chapter covers each arithmetic operator in MicroPython with detailed explanations and examples on the STM32 NUCLEO-F446RE.

Chapter Goal

- Understand and use basic arithmetic operators for mathematical calculations.
- Learn the syntax and behavior of each operator.
- Implement a practical project using arithmetic operators to perform real-time calculations.

Rules

- **Use Correct Operators for Calculations**: Choose the appropriate operator (e.g., +, -, *, /) based on the calculation type.
- **Avoid Integer Division When Decimal Results Are Needed**: Use / for floating-point division and // for integer-only results.
- **Apply Parentheses for Clarity**: Use parentheses to ensure calculations are performed in the correct order.
- **Combine Operators for Complex Calculations**: Chain operators in a single expression for more complex math.
- **Be Mindful of Division by Zero**: Division by zero raises an error; use conditions to prevent it.

Syntax Table

Serial No	Topic	Code Snippet	Simple Example
1	Addition	`result = a + b`	`sum = 10 + 5`
2	Subtraction	`result = a - b`	`difference = 10 - 5`
3	Multiplication	`result = a * b`	`product = 10 * 5`
4	Division	`result = a / b`	`quotient = 10 / 5`
5	Floor Division	`result = a // b`	`quotient = 10 // 3`
6	Modulus	`result = a % b`	`remainder = 10 % 3`
7	Exponentiation	`result = a ** b`	`power = 2 ** 3`
8	Using Parentheses	`result = (a + b) * c`	`total = (10 + 5) * 2`

Topic Explanations

1. Addition (+)

What is Addition?

The addition operator (+) adds two numbers together. It is one of the most basic operations and is used in many types of calculations, such as summing sensor readings or combining counts.

Use Purpose

- **Combine Values**: Used to add numerical values.
- **Summing Data**: Useful for totals and cumulative sums.

Syntax

```
result = a + b
```

Syntax Explanation

- **a + b**: Adds two values, a and b, and stores the result in `result`.
- **+ (Addition Operator)**: Performs addition between a and b.

Simple Code Example

```
a = 10
b = 5
sum_result = a + b   # Result is 15
```

Code Example Explanation

- **Adds 10 and 5**: The result, 15, is stored in `sum_result`.

Notes

- Addition can be used with both integers and floating-point numbers.
- Can be combined in complex expressions with other arithmetic operators.

Warnings

- Adding incompatible types (e.g., string + integer) raises a `TypeError`.

---

2. Subtraction (-)

What is Subtraction?

The subtraction operator (-) subtracts one number from another. It is commonly used for calculating differences, adjusting counts, and reducing values.

Use Purpose

- **Calculate Differences**: Finds the difference between values.
- **Decrease Counts**: Useful for reducing a total by a certain amount.

Syntax

```
result = a - b
```

Syntax Explanation

- **a - b**: Subtracts b from a and stores the result in `result`.
- **- (Subtraction Operator)**: Performs subtraction between a and b.

Simple Code Example

```
a = 10
b = 5
difference = a - b   # Result is 5
```

Code Example Explanation

- **Subtracts 5 from 10**: The result, 5, is stored in `difference`.

Notes

- Can be used with both integers and floats.
- Works in complex expressions with other operators.

Warnings

- Be cautious of negative results when subtracting smaller numbers from larger ones.

---

3. Multiplication (*)

What is Multiplication?

The multiplication operator (*) multiplies two numbers. It is used for scaling values, calculating products, and generating sequences.

Use Purpose
- **Calculate Products**: Finds the product of two values.
- **Scale Values**: Adjusts values by multiplying with a constant.

Syntax
```
result = a * b
```

Syntax Explanation
- **a * b**: Multiplies a and b and stores the result in `result`.
- *** (Multiplication Operator)**: Performs multiplication between a and b.

Simple Code Example
```
a = 10
b = 5
product = a * b   # Result is 50
```

Code Example Explanation
- **Multiplies 10 and 5**: The result, 50, is stored in `product`.

Notes
- Multiplication works with both integers and floats.
- Supports chained expressions, like a * b * c.

Warnings
- Multiplying large numbers may result in overflow, especially with integers.

---

4. Division (/)

What is Division?
The division operator (/) divides one number by another, yielding a floating-point result. It's commonly used in calculations that require precision, such as averaging values.

Use Purpose
- **Calculate Ratios**: Finds the ratio between two values.
- **Average Data**: Used in dividing sums to find averages.

Syntax

```
result = a / b
```

Syntax Explanation

- **a / b**: Divides a by b and stores the result in `result`.
- **/ (Division Operator)**: Performs division between a and b.

Simple Code Example

```
a = 10
b = 5
quotient = a / b   # Result is 2.0
```

Code Example Explanation

- **Divides 10 by 5**: The result, 2.0, is stored in `quotient`.

Notes

- Division always produces a float, even if both numbers are integers.
- Use // for integer division.

Warnings

- Dividing by zero raises a `ZeroDivisionError`.

---

5. Floor Division (//)

What is Floor Division?

The floor division operator (//) divides one number by another and rounds the result down to the nearest integer. This is useful when only the whole number portion of a division result is needed.

Use Purpose

- **Integer Division**: Find integer results without decimals.
- **Round Down Quotients**: Rounds results down to the nearest integer.

Syntax

```
result = a // b
```

Syntax Explanation
- **a // b**: Divides a by b and rounds down to the nearest integer.
- **// (Floor Division Operator)**: Performs integer division between a and b.

Simple Code Example
```
a = 10
b = 3
quotient = a // b   # Result is 3
```

Code Example Explanation
- **Divides 10 by 3**: The result, 3, is stored in `quotient`.

Notes
- Useful in loops or cases where decimals are not required.
- Can be combined with other operators in expressions.

Warnings
- Like regular division, dividing by zero raises a `ZeroDivisionError`.

---

6. Modulus (%)

What is Modulus?
The modulus operator (%) returns the remainder of a division. It's commonly used for determining if a number is even or odd and for cyclic calculations.

Use Purpose
- **Find Remainders**: Returns the remainder after division.
- **Check Even/Odd**: number % 2 == 0 for even numbers, number % 2 == 1 for odd numbers.

Syntax
```
result = a % b
```

Syntax Explanation

- **a % b**: Divides a by b and returns the remainder.
- **% (Modulus Operator)**: Finds the remainder of division.

Simple Code Example

```
a = 10
b = 3
remainder = a % b   # Result is 1
```

Code Example Explanation

- **Finds Remainder of 10 Divided by 3**: The result, 1, is stored in remainder.

Notes

- Often used to determine divisibility.
- Works with both integers and floats.

---

7. Exponentiation (**)

What is Exponentiation?

The exponentiation operator (**) raises a number to the power of another. This is commonly used in scientific calculations and generating powers.

Use Purpose

- **Calculate Powers**: Raise numbers to powers.
- **Square and Cube Values**: Calculate squares, cubes, and other powers.

Syntax

```
result = a ** b
```

Syntax Explanation

- **a ** b**: Raises a to the power of b and stores the result in result.
- **** (Exponentiation Operator)**: Performs exponentiation on a and b.

Simple Code Example

```
a = 2
b = 3
power = a ** b   # Result is 8
```

Code Example Explanation

- **Calculates 2 Raised to the Power of 3**: The result, 8, is stored in power.

Notes

- Exponentiation supports both integer and floating-point values.
- Useful in scientific and mathematical applications.

Warnings

- Large exponents may result in overflow.

8. Using Parentheses for Order of Operations

What is the Purpose of Parentheses?

Parentheses group expressions to control the order of operations. This is essential when combining multiple operators, as it clarifies which calculations are performed first.

Use Purpose

- **Control Calculation Order**: Ensure calculations happen in the intended sequence.
- **Improve Readability**: Clearly indicates priority in expressions.

Syntax

```
result = (a + b) * c
```

Syntax Explanation

- **(a + b)**: Parentheses around a + b ensure this operation is performed first.
- *** c**: Multiplies the result of (a + b) by c.

Simple Code Example

```
a = 10
b = 5
c = 2
total = (a + b) * c  # Result is 30
```

Code Example Explanation

- **Adds a and b First, Then Multiplies by c**: $(10 + 5) * 2$ results in 30.

Notes

- Parentheses override the default operator precedence.
- Helps avoid logic errors in complex expressions.

Warnings

- Too many nested parentheses can reduce readability.

Final Project: Real-Time Arithmetic Calculations Using Sensors

Project Objective

Use a potentiometer as an input to perform real-time arithmetic calculations and control the brightness of an LED based on sensor values.

Project Circuit

Component	STM32 Pin	Connection Details
Potentiometer	A1	Connect one end to 3.3V, the other to GND, and wiper to A1
LED with Resistor	A2	Connect LED to A2 with a resistor, and the other end to GND

Project Code

```python
from machine import ADC, Pin, PWM
import time

# Initialize potentiometer on ADC pin A1
potentiometer = ADC(Pin("A1"))

# Initialize LED on PWM pin A2
led_pwm = PWM(Pin("A2"), freq=1000)

while True:
    # Read sensor value
    sensor_value = potentiometer.read_u16()

    # Scale sensor value to 0-100 for percentage
    percentage = (sensor_value / 65535) * 100
    brightness = int((percentage / 100) * 65535)  # Scale brightness

    # Display calculations
    print(f"Sensor Value: {sensor_value}, Percentage:
{percentage:.2f}%, Brightness: {brightness}")

    # Set LED brightness
    led_pwm.duty_u16(brightness)

    # Delay for stability
    time.sleep(0.1)
```

Save and Run

1. Save this code as main.py on your STM32 NUCLEO.
2. Run the script; turning the potentiometer will adjust the LED brightness, with calculations displayed in real-time.

Check Output

The LED brightness should increase or decrease as you adjust the potentiometer, with the sensor value and brightness calculations printed to the console.

Comparison Operators in STM32

Chapter Overview

Comparison operators are used to compare values and determine relationships, such as equality, greater-than, or less-than conditions. These operators are essential for controlling program flow and decision-making, especially in conditional statements and loops. This chapter covers each comparison operator in MicroPython for STM32 with detailed syntax, examples, and a practical project.

Chapter Goal

- Understand and use comparison operators to evaluate expressions.
- Learn the syntax and behavior of each comparison operator.
- Implement a practical project using comparison operators to control hardware based on sensor data.

Rules

- **Use Comparison Operators for Decision-Making**: Apply these operators in conditions to control program flow based on relationships.
- **Combine with Logical Operators**: Use logical operators to evaluate multiple comparisons simultaneously.
- **Avoid Unnecessary Comparisons**: Only compare values when necessary to maintain efficiency.
- **Ensure Compatible Data Types**: Use comparison operators on compatible data types to avoid errors.
- **Use Comparison Results in Conditions**: Comparison operators return booleans, which can be used directly in `if`, `while`, and other conditional statements.

Syntax Table

Serial No	Topic	Code Snippet	Simple Example
1	Equal to (==)	result = a == b	is_equal = (10 == 5)
2	Not equal to (!=)	result = a != b	not_equal = (10 != 5)
3	Greater than (>)	result = a > b	is_greater = (10 > 5)
4	Less than (<)	result = a < b	is_less = (10 < 5)
5	Greater than or equal to (>=)	result = a >= b	is_greater_equal = (10 >= 5)
6	Less than or equal to (<=)	result = a <= b	is_less_equal = (10 <= 5)
7	Using Comparison in if	if a == b:	if sensor_value == target:

Topic Explanations

1. Equal to (==)

What is ==?

The == operator checks if two values are equal. It returns True if the values are the same, and False otherwise. This operator is often used to confirm a specific condition or state in conditional statements.

Use Purpose

- **Check Equality**: Used to verify if two values are identical.
- **Control Flow**: Often used in `if` statements to branch code execution.

Syntax

```
result = a == b
```

Syntax Explanation

- **a == b**: Compares a and b for equality.
- **== (Equal to Operator)**: Returns `True` if a and b are equal; `False` otherwise.

Simple Code Example

```
a = 10
b = 5
is_equal = (a == b)  # Result is False
```

Code Example Explanation

- **Compares 10 and 5**: Since 10 is not equal to 5, `is_equal` is set to `False`.

Notes

- `==` can be used with numbers, strings, booleans, and other compatible data types.
- Commonly used in conditional statements.

Warnings

- Do not confuse == (equality) with = (assignment).

---

2. Not equal to (!=)

What is !=?

The `!=` operator checks if two values are not equal. It returns `True` if the values are different, and `False` if they are the same.

Use Purpose

- **Check Inequality**: Used to determine if two values are not identical.
- **Control Flow**: Commonly used to handle cases where values differ.

Syntax

```
result = a != b
```

Syntax Explanation

- **a != b**: Checks if a and b are not equal.
- **!= (Not Equal to Operator)**: Returns True if a and b are not equal; False otherwise.

Simple Code Example

```
a = 10
b = 5
not_equal = (a != b)  # Result is True
```

Code Example Explanation

- **Compares 10 and 5**: Since 10 is not equal to 5, not_equal is True.

Notes

- != can be used with various data types, including numbers and strings.
- Often used in loops and conditions.

Warnings

- Do not use != with data types that cannot be directly compared, as it may cause errors.

3. Greater than (>)

What is >?

The > operator checks if one value is greater than another. It returns True if the left operand is greater, and False otherwise.

Use Purpose

- **Compare Sizes**: Used to compare numerical values or quantities.
- **Filter Data**: Often used to filter values that exceed a threshold.

Syntax

```
result = a > b
```

Syntax Explanation

- **a > b**: Checks if a is greater than b.
- **> (Greater Than Operator)**: Returns True if a is greater than b; False otherwise.

Simple Code Example

```
a = 10
b = 5
is_greater = (a > b)  # Result is True
```

Code Example Explanation

- **Compares 10 and 5**: Since 10 is greater than 5, is_greater is True.

Notes

- Can be used with both integers and floating-point numbers.
- Useful in conditions and loops for filtering data.

Warnings

- Comparing incompatible data types, like integers and strings, may cause errors.

4. Less than (<)

What is <?

The < operator checks if one value is less than another. It returns True if the left operand is smaller, and False otherwise.

Use Purpose

- **Compare Quantities**: Used to determine if a value is below a certain threshold.
- **Set Limits**: Often used to ensure values remain within a specified range.

Syntax

```
result = a < b
```

Syntax Explanation

- **a < b**: Checks if a is less than b.
- **< (Less Than Operator)**: Returns True if a is less than b; False otherwise.

Simple Code Example

```
a = 10
b = 5
is_less = (a < b)  # Result is False
```

Code Example Explanation

- **Compares 10 and 5**: Since 10 is not less than 5, is_less is False.

Notes

- Works with integers, floats, and other comparable types.
- Often used in conditional statements and loops.

Warnings

- Ensure values are of compatible types when using <.

5. Greater than or equal to (>=)

What is >=?

The >= operator checks if one value is greater than or equal to another. It returns True if the left operand is greater or equal, and False otherwise.

Use Purpose

- **Set Minimum Requirements**: Used to ensure values meet or exceed a threshold.
- **Control Flow**: Allows branching based on whether values reach a certain level.

Syntax

```
result = a >= b
```

Syntax Explanation

- **a >= b**: Checks if a is greater than or equal to b.
- **>= (Greater Than or Equal to Operator)**: Returns True if a is greater than or equal to b; False otherwise.

Simple Code Example

```
a = 10
b = 5
is_greater_equal = (a >= b)  # Result is True
```

Code Example Explanation

- **Compares 10 and 5**: Since 10 is greater than 5, is_greater_equal is True.

Notes

- Useful in loops or conditions that allow a minimum value.
- Can be combined with logical operators to form complex conditions.

Warnings

- Avoid comparing incompatible types, as this can lead to errors.

6. Less than or equal to (<=)

What is <=?

The <= operator checks if one value is less than or equal to another. It returns True if the left operand is smaller or equal, and False otherwise.

Use Purpose

- **Set Maximum Limits**: Useful for enforcing upper boundaries.
- **Control Flow**: Commonly used in conditional statements to check if a value is within limits.

Syntax

```
result = a <= b
```

Syntax Explanation

- **a <= b**: Checks if a is less than or equal to b.
- **<= (Less Than or Equal to Operator)**: Returns True if a is less than or equal to b; False otherwise.

Simple Code Example

```
a = 10
b = 5
is_less_equal = (a <= b)  # Result is False
```

Code Example Explanation

- **Compares 10 and 5**: Since 10 is not less than or equal to 5, is_less_equal is False.

Notes

- Frequently used in loops or conditions where a maximum limit is required.
- Can be combined with other operators for complex checks.

Warnings

- Ensure compatible data types to avoid errors.

7. Using Comparison in `if`

What is Comparison in `if`?

Comparison operators are often used directly in `if` statements to evaluate conditions and control program flow. The `if` statement will execute the code block only if the comparison condition is `True`.

Use Purpose

- **Control Program Flow**: Allows branching based on specific conditions.
- **Evaluate Conditions**: Used in control structures like `if`, `while`, and loops.

Syntax

```
if a == b:
    # Code to execute if a equals b
```

Syntax Explanation

- **if**: Starts the conditional statement.
- **a == b**: Condition to check if a equals b.
- **: (Colon)**: Starts the indented block for the `if` statement.
- **Indented Block**: Code executed if the condition is `True`.

Simple Code Example

```
sensor_value = 500
target = 500
if sensor_value == target:
    print("Sensor is at target value.")
```

Code Example Explanation

- **Checks if Sensor Value Matches Target**: If `sensor_value` is equal to `target`, it prints "Sensor is at target value."

Notes

- Comparison conditions in `if` statements determine which code executes.
- Can be combined with `elif` and `else` for more complex branching.

Warnings

- Ensure conditions are logically correct to avoid unintended behavior.

Final Project: Sensor-Controlled LED with Comparison Operators

Project Objective

Create a program that reads a potentiometer's value and adjusts an LED's brightness based on specific threshold comparisons.

Project Circuit

Component	STM3 2 Pin	Connection Details
Potentiometer	A1	Connect one end to 3.3V, the other to GND, and wiper to A1
LED with Resistor	A2	Connect LED to A2 with a resistor, and the other end to GND

Project Code

```
from machine import ADC, Pin, PWM
import time

# Initialize potentiometer on ADC pin A1
potentiometer = ADC(Pin("A1"))

# Initialize LED on PWM pin A2
led_pwm = PWM(Pin("A2"), freq=1000)

while True:
```

```python
    # Read sensor value
    sensor_value = potentiometer.read_u16()

    # Adjust brightness based on sensor value thresholds
    if sensor_value < 20000:
        brightness = 0   # LED off
    elif sensor_value < 40000:
        brightness = 32768  # Half brightness
    else:
        brightness = 65535  # Full brightness

    # Set LED brightness
    led_pwm.duty_u16(brightness)

    # Display sensor value and brightness level
    print(f"Sensor Value: {sensor_value}, LED Brightness:
{brightness}")

    # Delay for stability
    time.sleep(0.1)
```

Save and Run

1. Save this code as main.py on your STM32 NUCLEO.
2. Run the script; turning the potentiometer will adjust the LED's brightness based on predefined thresholds.

Check Output

As you adjust the potentiometer, the LED will turn off, dim to half brightness, or illuminate at full brightness based on the sensor value thresholds.

Boolean Operators in STM32

Chapter Overview

Boolean operators are used to perform logical operations, allowing a program to make decisions based on multiple conditions. They include operators like and, or, and not, which help control program flow in conditional statements. Boolean operators are essential for implementing complex conditions and enabling decision-making. This chapter covers each Boolean operator in MicroPython for STM32 with detailed syntax, examples, and a practical project.

Chapter Goal

- Understand and use Boolean operators to evaluate complex conditions.
- Learn the syntax and behavior of each Boolean operator.
- Implement a practical project using Boolean operators to control hardware based on combined sensor data.

Rules

- **Use and to Require Multiple Conditions**: Use and when all conditions need to be True for the entire expression to be True.
- **Use or to Allow Any Condition**: Use or when at least one condition needs to be True for the expression to be True.
- **Use not to Invert Conditions**: Use not to negate or invert a condition, turning True to False and vice versa.
- **Combine Boolean Operators**: Combine and, or, and not for complex logical expressions.
- **Use Parentheses for Clarity**: When using multiple Boolean operators, use parentheses to ensure the correct order of operations.

Syntax Table

Seria l No	Topic	Code Snippet	Simple Example
1	and Operator	`result = condition1 and condition2`	`is_valid = (age > 18 and has_license)`
2	or Operator	`result = condition1 or condition2`	`can_enter = (age >= 18 or with_parent)`
3	not Operator	`result = not condition`	`is_minor = not (age >= 18)`
4	Combining Boolean Operators	`(condition1 and condition2) or condition3`	`(age > 18 and has_license) or with_supervisor`
5	Using Boolean Operators in if	`if (condition1 and condition2):`	`if (sensor1 > 500 and sensor2 < 500):`

Topic Explanations

1. and Operator

What is the and Operator?

The and operator checks if multiple conditions are all True. It returns True only if all conditions connected by and are True; otherwise, it returns False.

Use Purpose

- **Require All Conditions**: Use and when all conditions must be met for the result to be True.
- **Combine Conditions**: Enables multiple requirements in a single expression.

Syntax

```
result = condition1 and condition2
```

Syntax Explanation

- **condition1 and condition2**: Evaluates to True if both condition1 and condition2 are True.
- **and (Logical AND Operator)**: Connects two conditions, resulting in True only if both conditions are met.

Simple Code Example

```
age = 20
has_license = True
is_valid_driver = (age >= 18 and has_license)  # Result is True
```

Code Example Explanation

- **Checks Age and License**: The is_valid_driver variable is True only if age is at least 18 and has_license is True.

Notes

- The and operator short-circuits, meaning it stops evaluating as soon as one condition is False.
- Useful in if statements to check multiple conditions at once.

Warnings

- Ensure all conditions are compatible with logical evaluation, as incompatible types may cause errors.

---

2. or Operator

What is the or Operator?

The or operator checks if at least one of multiple conditions is True. It returns True if any condition is True, and only returns False if all conditions are False.

Use Purpose

- **Allow Any Condition**: Use or when any one of multiple conditions can satisfy the requirement.
- **Combine Alternative Conditions**: Enables flexibility by accepting any one of multiple conditions.

Syntax

```
result = condition1 or condition2
```

Syntax Explanation

- **condition1 or condition2**: Evaluates to True if either condition1 or condition2 is True.
- **or (Logical OR Operator)**: Connects two conditions, resulting in True if at least one condition is met.

Simple Code Example

```
age = 16
with_parent = True
can_enter = (age >= 18 or with_parent)  # Result is True
```

Code Example Explanation

- **Checks Age or Parental Supervision**: The can_enter variable is True if either age is at least 18 or with_parent is True.

Notes

- The or operator short-circuits, meaning it stops evaluating as soon as one condition is True.
- Useful in conditions where any one of several conditions can allow code execution.

Warnings

- Be cautious when combining multiple or operators, as it can make conditions difficult to read.

3. not Operator

What is the not Operator?

The not operator inverts a condition's value, changing True to False and False to True.

Use Purpose

- **Invert Conditions**: Use not to reverse a condition, especially in if statements.
- **Toggle Boolean Values**: Can be used to flip a boolean value for conditions or flags.

Syntax

```
result = not condition
```

Syntax Explanation

- **not condition**: Evaluates to True if condition is False, and to False if condition is True.
- **not (Logical NOT Operator)**: Inverts the condition's boolean value.

Simple Code Example

```
age = 15
is_minor = not (age >= 18)   # Result is True
```

Code Example Explanation

- **Checks if Minor**: The is_minor variable is True if age is less than 18.

Notes

- not is often used with other Boolean operators to create complex expressions.
- Use parentheses with not to clarify which condition is being negated.

4. Combining Boolean Operators

What is Combining Boolean Operators?

Boolean operators can be combined to create complex conditions. Combining and, or, and not allows for detailed and precise control of conditions.

Use Purpose

- **Create Complex Conditions**: Enables multiple criteria to be evaluated together.
- **Precise Logic Control**: Allows for specific conditions that require multiple checks.

Syntax

```
result = (condition1 and condition2) or condition3
```

Syntax Explanation

- **(condition1 and condition2) or condition3**: Combines and and or operators, evaluated based on parentheses.
- **Logical Operators**: Combine multiple Boolean operators in a single expression for detailed conditions.

Simple Code Example

```
age = 20
has_license = True
with_supervisor = False
can_drive = (age >= 18 and has_license) or with_supervisor  # Result is
True
```

Code Example Explanation

- **Checks Multiple Conditions for Driving**: can_drive is True if age is at least 18 and has_license is True, or if with_supervisor is True.

Notes

- Use parentheses to clarify the order of operations when combining Boolean operators.
- Complex conditions are often used in if statements.

5. Using Boolean Operators in `if`

What is Using Boolean Operators in `if`?

Boolean operators are commonly used in `if` statements to control program flow based on multiple conditions.

Use Purpose

- **Direct Program Flow**: Controls which code executes based on logical conditions.
- **Evaluate Multiple Criteria**: Allows multiple conditions to influence the program's path.

Syntax

```
if (condition1 and condition2):
    # Code to execute if both conditions are True
```

Syntax Explanation

- **if (condition1 and condition2)**: Evaluates if both conditions are True.
- **: (Colon)**: Starts the indented block for the `if` statement.
- **Indented Block**: Code executed if the conditions are met.

Simple Code Example

```
sensor1 = 600
sensor2 = 400
if (sensor1 > 500 and sensor2 < 500):
    print("Sensor values are within the desired range.")
```

Code Example Explanation

- **Checks Sensor Values**: The message prints only if `sensor1` is greater than 500 and `sensor2` is less than 500.

Notes

- Boolean operators in `if` statements allow for flexible and precise control over code execution.
- Parentheses can clarify the order of operations and prevent logic errors.

Final Project: Dual-Sensor Controlled LED Using Boolean Operators

Project Objective

Create a program that reads values from two sensors and adjusts an LED's brightness based on specific conditions involving Boolean operators.

Project Circuit

Component	STM 32 Pin	Connection Details
Potentiometer 1	A1	Connect one end to 3.3V, the other to GND, and wiper to A1
Potentiometer 2	A2	Connect one end to 3.3V, the other to GND, and wiper to A2
LED with Resistor	A3	Connect LED to A3 with a resistor, and the other end to GND

Project Code

```
from machine import ADC, Pin, PWM
import time

# Initialize potentiometers on ADC pins A1 and A2
pot1 = ADC(Pin("A1"))
pot2 = ADC(Pin("A2"))

# Initialize LED on PWM pin A3
led_pwm = PWM(Pin("A3"), freq=1000)

while True:
    # Read values from both potentiometers
    sensor1_value = pot1.read_u16()
    sensor2_value = pot2.read_u16()

    # Apply Boolean logic to adjust LED brightness
    if (sensor1_value > 30000 and sensor2_value > 30000):
        brightness = 65535  # Full brightness
    elif (sensor1_value > 20000 or sensor2_value > 20000):
```

```
        brightness = 32768  # Medium brightness
    else:
        brightness = 0  # LED off

    # Set LED brightness
    led_pwm.duty_u16(brightness)

    # Display sensor values and LED brightness level
    print(f"Sensor1: {sensor1_value}, Sensor2: {sensor2_value}, LED
Brightness: {brightness}")

    # Delay for stability
    time.sleep(0.1)
```

Save and Run

1. Save this code as main.py on your STM32 NUCLEO.
2. Run the script; adjusting the potentiometers will change the LED's brightness based on predefined Boolean logic conditions.

Check Output

The LED brightness should change according to the combined sensor readings:

- Full brightness when both sensors are above 30000.
- Medium brightness when either sensor is above 20000.
- LED off when both sensors are below 20000.

Compound Operators in STM32 NUCLEO-F446RE with MicroPython

Chapter Overview

Compound operators (also known as augmented assignment operators) combine an arithmetic operation with assignment, making it easy to update the value of a variable without rewriting the variable name. These operators streamline code, particularly in loops and iterative calculations. This chapter covers each compound operator in MicroPython for STM32 with detailed syntax, examples, and a practical project.

Chapter Goal

- Understand and use compound operators to simplify calculations.
- Learn the syntax and behavior of each compound operator.
- Implement a practical project using compound operators to control hardware based on iterative calculations.

Rules

- **Use Compound Operators for Efficiency**: Compound operators simplify code by combining arithmetic and assignment in a single step.
- **Choose the Right Operator**: Use +=, -=, *=, /=, //=, %=, and **= based on the type of calculation.
- **Use in Loops and Iterations**: Compound operators are particularly useful in loops for updating values.
- **Be Mindful of Data Types**: Ensure compatibility with the data type of the variable to avoid errors.
- **Avoid Overuse in Complex Expressions**: Excessive use can make code harder to read if overused in complex calculations.

Syntax Table

Serial No	Topic	Code Snippet	Simple Example
1	Addition Assignment (+=)	`variable += value`	`counter += 1`
2	Subtraction Assignment (-=)	`variable -= value`	`balance -= 100`
3	Multiplication Assignment (*=)	`variable *= value`	`total *= 2`
4	Division Assignment (/=)	`variable /= value`	`average /= 10`
5	Floor Division Assignment (//=)	`variable //= value`	`num_items //= 3`
6	Modulus Assignment (%=)	`variable %= value`	`remainder %= 4`
7	Exponentiation Assignment (**=)	`variable **= value`	`power **= 2`

Topic Explanations

1. Addition Assignment (+=)

What is Addition Assignment?

The addition assignment operator (+=) adds a specified value to a variable and then assigns the result back to the same variable. It is commonly used for counters and cumulative sums.

Use Purpose

- **Increment Counters**: Efficiently increases counters or accumulates totals.
- **Simplify Accumulation**: Adds values to a variable without repeating the variable name.

Syntax

```
variable += value
```

Syntax Explanation

- **variable += value**: Adds `value` to `variable` and assigns the result back to `variable`.
- **+= (Addition Assignment Operator)**: Combines addition and assignment.

Simple Code Example

```
counter = 0
counter += 1   # Result is 1
```

Code Example Explanation

- **Increments Counter**: Adds 1 to `counter`, updating its value to 1.

Notes

- Works with integers, floats, and strings (for concatenation).
- Often used in loops and iterative processes.

Warnings

- Using += on incompatible types (e.g., int and string) will raise a `TypeError`.

---

2. Subtraction Assignment (-=)

What is Subtraction Assignment?

The subtraction assignment operator (-=) subtracts a specified value from a variable and assigns the result back to the same variable.

Use Purpose

- **Decrement Counters**: Efficiently decreases counters or reduces totals.
- **Simplify Reduction**: Reduces values in a variable without repeating the variable name.

Syntax

```
variable -= value
```

Syntax Explanation

- **variable -= value**: Subtracts value from variable and assigns the result back to variable.
- **-= (Subtraction Assignment Operator)**: Combines subtraction and assignment.

Simple Code Example

```
balance = 1000
balance -= 100  # Result is 900
```

Code Example Explanation

- **Decreases Balance**: Subtracts 100 from balance, updating it to 900.

Notes

- Works with both integers and floats.
- Commonly used in loops and conditional statements.

Warnings

- Ensure compatible types to avoid errors.

---

3. Multiplication Assignment (*=)

What is Multiplication Assignment?

The multiplication assignment operator (*=) multiplies a variable by a specified value and assigns the result back to the variable.

Use Purpose

- **Scale Values**: Useful for scaling values or calculations requiring repeated multiplication.
- **Simplify Multiplication**: Multiplies a variable by a factor without repeating the variable name.

Syntax

```
variable *= value
```

Syntax Explanation

- *variable* = *value*: Multiplies `variable` by `value` and assigns the result back to `variable`.
- ***= (Multiplication Assignment Operator)**: Combines multiplication and assignment.

Simple Code Example

```
total = 50
total *= 2   # Result is 100
```

Code Example Explanation

- **Doubles Total**: Multiplies `total` by 2, updating it to 100.

Notes

- Works with both integers and floats.
- Can be used to calculate exponential growth in loops.

Warnings

- Multiplying large numbers may lead to overflow in certain data types.

---

4. Division Assignment (/=)

What is Division Assignment?

The division assignment operator (/=) divides a variable by a specified value and assigns the result back to the variable. This operation always produces a floating-point result.

Use Purpose

- **Divide Totals**: Useful for averaging or reducing values in iterative calculations.
- **Simplify Division**: Divides a variable by a divisor without repeating the variable name.

Syntax

```
variable /= value
```

Syntax Explanation

- **variable /= value**: Divides `variable` by `value` and assigns the result back to `variable`.
- **/= (Division Assignment Operator)**: Combines division and assignment.

Simple Code Example

```
average = 100
average /= 10   # Result is 10.0
```

Code Example Explanation

- **Calculates Average**: Divides `average` by 10, updating it to 10.0.

Notes

- Always produces a float, even if both operands are integers.
- Commonly used in loops for averaging calculations.

Warnings

- Dividing by zero raises a `ZeroDivisionError`.

---

5. Floor Division Assignment (//=)

What is Floor Division Assignment?

The floor division assignment operator (//=) divides a variable by a specified value and rounds the result down to the nearest integer, assigning the result back to the variable.

Use Purpose

- **Integer Division**: Useful for situations where only the whole number part of the division result is needed.
- **Simplify Floor Division**: Divides a variable by a value and discards any decimals without repeating the variable name.

Syntax

```
variable //= value
```

Syntax Explanation

- **variable //= value**: Divides `variable` by `value`, rounds down, and assigns the result back to `variable`.
- **//= (Floor Division Assignment Operator)**: Combines floor division and assignment.

Simple Code Example

```
num_items = 10
num_items //= 3   # Result is 3
```

Code Example Explanation

- **Calculates Integer Quotient**: Divides `num_items` by 3 and rounds down to 3.

Notes

- Works with integers and floats, but always rounds down the result.
- Commonly used in cases where fractional results are not needed.

Warnings

- Ensure the divisor is not zero, as this raises a `ZeroDivisionError`.

---

6. Modulus Assignment (%=)

What is Modulus Assignment?

The modulus assignment operator (%=) finds the remainder when a variable is divided by a specified value and assigns the result back to the variable.

Use Purpose

- **Calculate Remainders**: Useful for cyclic calculations and determining divisibility.
- **Simplify Modulus Calculation**: Finds the remainder without repeating the variable name.

Syntax

```
variable %= value
```

Syntax Explanation

- **variable %= value**: Calculates `variable` modulo `value` and assigns the remainder back to `variable`.
- **%= (Modulus Assignment Operator)**: Combines modulus and assignment.

Simple Code Example

```
remainder = 10
remainder %= 3   # Result is 1
```

Code Example Explanation

- **Finds Remainder of 10 Divided by 3**: The result, 1, is stored in `remainder`.

Notes

- Commonly used in cyclic calculations, such as counting in loops.
- Useful for checking divisibility and patterns.

Warnings

- Dividing by zero with %= raises a `ZeroDivisionError`.

---

7. Exponentiation Assignment (**=)

What is Exponentiation Assignment?

The exponentiation assignment operator (**=) raises a variable to the power of a specified value and assigns the result back to the variable.

Use Purpose

- **Calculate Powers**: Useful for calculations requiring exponentiation.
- **Simplify Exponentiation**: Raises a variable to a power without repeating the variable name.

Syntax

```
variable **= value
```

Syntax Explanation

- ****variable = value**: Raises `variable` to the power of `value` and assigns the result back to `variable`.
- ****= (Exponentiation Assignment Operator)**: Combines exponentiation and assignment.

Simple Code Example

```
power = 2
power **= 3  # Result is 8
```

Code Example Explanation

- **Calculates Power of 2 Raised to 3**: `power` is updated to 8.

Notes

- Useful for scientific calculations and growth patterns.
- Supports both integers and floats.

Project: LED Brightness Control with Iterative Calculations

Create a program that adjusts an LED's brightness based on sensor readings, using compound operators to iteratively change the brightness level based on user-defined increments.

Project Circuit

Component	STM32 Pin	Connection Details
Potentiometer	A1	Connect one end to 3.3V, the other to GND, and wiper to A1
LED with Resistor	A2	Connect LED to A2 with a resistor, and the other end to GND

Project Code

```python
from machine import ADC, Pin, PWM
import time

# Initialize potentiometer on ADC pin A1
potentiometer = ADC(Pin("A1"))

# Initialize LED on PWM pin A2
led_pwm = PWM(Pin("A2"), freq=1000)

# Set initial brightness and increment value
brightness = 0
increment = 5000

while True:
    # Read sensor value
    sensor_value = potentiometer.read_u16()

    # Adjust brightness based on sensor value
    if sensor_value > 40000:
        brightness += increment  # Increase brightness
    elif sensor_value < 20000:
        brightness -= increment  # Decrease brightness

    # Cap brightness within 0 to max PWM range
    if brightness > 65535:
        brightness = 65535
    elif brightness < 0:
        brightness = 0

    # Set LED brightness
    led_pwm.duty_u16(brightness)

    # Display sensor value and brightness level
    print(f"Sensor Value: {sensor_value}, LED Brightness:
{brightness}")

    # Delay for stability
    time.sleep(0.1)
```

Save and Run

1. Save this code as main.py on your STM32 NUCLEO.
2. Run the script; turning the potentiometer will dynamically adjust the LED's brightness using the compound operators.

Check Output

The LED brightness will increase or decrease based on the potentiometer's position, with adjustments handled through compound operators.

Bitwise Operators in STM32

Chapter Overview

Bitwise operators perform operations directly on the binary representations of integers, making them powerful tools for low-level programming and hardware control. They include operators like AND, OR, XOR, NOT, shift left, and shift right, and are useful for tasks such as setting or clearing specific bits in registers, performing quick calculations, and handling flags. This chapter covers each bitwise operator in MicroPython for STM32 with detailed syntax, examples, and a practical project.

Chapter Goal

- Understand and use bitwise operators to perform binary operations.
- Learn the syntax and behavior of each bitwise operator.
- Implement a practical project using bitwise operators to manipulate LED patterns based on binary inputs.

Rules

- **Use Bitwise Operators for Low-Level Control**: Apply these operators when direct bit manipulation is needed.
- **Choose Operators Carefully**: Select the correct operator based on the type of manipulation, such as masking with & or setting bits with |.
- **Combine Operators for Complex Bit Manipulations**: Bitwise operators can be combined to perform complex bit manipulations.
- **Ensure Compatibility with Integer Types**: Bitwise operations work only on integers, so avoid using other data types.
- **Use Binary Representation for Clarity**: When working with bitwise operators, binary literals can make code clearer and easier to debug.

Syntax Table

Serial No	Topic	Code Snippet	Simple Example
1	Bitwise AND (&)	`result = a & b`	`masked = value & 0x0F`
2	Bitwise OR (`` ` ``)	`` ` ``)	`` ` ``result = a
3	Bitwise XOR (^)	`result = a ^ b`	`toggle = value ^ 0xFF`
4	Bitwise NOT (~)	`result = ~a`	`inverted = ~value`
5	Left Shift (<<)	`result = a << n`	`shifted = value << 2`
6	Right Shift (>>)	`result = a >> n`	`shifted = value >> 1`

Topic Explanations

1. Bitwise AND (&)

What is Bitwise AND?

The bitwise AND operator (&) compares each bit of two integers and returns 1 if both corresponding bits are 1; otherwise, it returns 0. This operator is often used for masking bits.

Use Purpose

- **Mask Specific Bits**: Used to isolate certain bits in a value.
- **Clear Bits**: Clears specific bits by ANDing with 0s.

Syntax

```
result = a & b
```

Syntax Explanation

- **a & b**: Compares the binary bits of a and b, keeping only the bits where both are 1.
- **& (Bitwise AND Operator)**: Performs bitwise AND between two integers.

Simple Code Example

```
value = 0b1101   # Binary: 1101
mask = 0b0101    # Binary: 0101
masked = value & mask   # Result is 0b0101 (binary 0101, decimal 5)
```

Code Example Explanation

- **Masks Value**: Only the bits where both `value` and `mask` are 1 remain in the result.

Notes

- Commonly used in embedded programming for isolating bits.
- Bitwise AND with `0x0F` often masks the lower 4 bits of a byte.

Warnings

- Ensure both operands are integers for compatibility.

---

2. Bitwise OR (|)

What is Bitwise OR?

The bitwise OR operator (|) compares each bit of two integers and returns 1 if either bit is 1. It's often used to set specific bits in a value.

Use Purpose

- **Set Specific Bits**: Used to turn on specific bits without changing other bits.
- **Combine Flags**: Used to merge bit flags or settings.

Syntax

```
result = a | b
```

Syntax Explanation

- **a | b**: Compares the binary bits of a and b, setting each bit to 1 if either is 1.
- **| (Bitwise OR Operator)**: Performs bitwise OR between two integers.

Simple Code Example

```
value = 0b0101   # Binary: 0101
mask = 0b1000    # Binary: 1000
combined = value | mask   # Result is 0b1101 (binary 1101, decimal 13)
```

Code Example Explanation

- **Sets Specific Bits**: The `combined` result has both bits set from `value` and `mask`.

Notes

- Commonly used to set control flags in a register.
- Bitwise OR with `0xF0` often sets the upper 4 bits of a byte.

Warnings

- Ensure operands are integers for correct operation.

---

3. Bitwise XOR (^)

What is Bitwise XOR?

The bitwise XOR operator (^) compares each bit of two integers and returns 1 if the bits are different. This operator is useful for toggling bits.

Use Purpose

- **Toggle Specific Bits**: Changes specific bits without affecting others.
- **Error Detection**: Commonly used in checksum and error detection algorithms.

Syntax

```
result = a ^ b
```

Syntax Explanation

- **a ^ b**: Compares the binary bits of a and b, setting each bit to 1 if they are different.
- **^ (Bitwise XOR Operator)**: Performs bitwise XOR between two integers.

Simple Code Example

```
value = 0b1010  # Binary: 1010
toggle = value ^ 0b1111  # Result is 0b0101 (binary 0101, decimal 5)
```

Code Example Explanation

- **Toggles Bits**: The XOR operation with 0b1111 inverts each bit.

Notes

- Useful for bit toggling and parity checks.
- XORing a value with itself results in 0.

Warnings

- Make sure both operands are integers.

---

4. Bitwise NOT (~)

What is Bitwise NOT?

The bitwise NOT operator (~) inverts each bit in an integer, turning 1s into 0s and 0s into 1s. This operation returns the two's complement of the integer, which effectively negates it.

Use Purpose

- **Invert Bits**: Used to flip all bits in a binary value.
- **Negate Integer**: Negates a number by returning its two's complement.

Syntax

```
result = ~a
```

Syntax Explanation

- **~a**: Inverts each bit in a.
- **~ (Bitwise NOT Operator)**: Flips all bits, turning 1s to 0s and 0s to 1s.

Simple Code Example

```
value = 0b0101   # Binary: 0101
inverted = ~value   # Result is -0b0110 (two's complement of 0b1010)
```

Code Example Explanation

- **Inverts Bits**: The NOT operation flips each bit in `value`.

Notes

- Inverts the number to its two's complement, so ~5 results in -6.
- Use carefully, as it changes the sign and value of the integer.

Warnings

- The output is the two's complement, which may not be intuitive for unsigned bit patterns.

---

5. Left Shift (<<)

What is Left Shift?

The left shift operator (<<) shifts the bits of a number to the left by a specified number of positions, effectively multiplying the number by powers of 2.

Use Purpose

- **Multiply by Powers of 2**: Shifts bits to the left, increasing the value by powers of 2.
- **Set Bits in Positions**: Used to set specific bits in bitmasks.

Syntax

```
result = a << n
```

Syntax Explanation

- **a << n**: Shifts a to the left by n bits, adding n zeros to the right.
- **<< (Left Shift Operator)**: Moves bits to the left, multiplying the value by 2^n.

Simple Code Example

```
value = 0b0001  # Binary: 0001
shifted = value << 2  # Result is 0b0100 (binary 0100, decimal 4)
```

Code Example Explanation

- **Shifts Left by 2**: The result, 0b0100, is 4 in decimal.

Notes

- Commonly used for multiplying by powers of 2.
- Shifting left by 1 multiplies the number by 2.

Warnings

- Shifting too far can result in overflow in some systems.

---

6. Right Shift (>>)

What is Right Shift?

The right shift operator (>>) shifts the bits of a number to the right by a specified number of positions, effectively dividing the number by powers of 2.

Use Purpose

- **Divide by Powers of 2**: Shifts bits to the right, decreasing the value by powers of 2.
- **Clear Least Significant Bits**: Often used to truncate or remove specific bits.

Syntax

```
result = a >> n
```

Syntax Explanation

- **a >> n**: Shifts a to the right by n bits, discarding n bits from the right.
- **>> (Right Shift Operator)**: Moves bits to the right, dividing the value by 2^n.

Simple Code Example

```
value = 0b1000  # Binary: 1000
shifted = value >> 2  # Result is 0b0010 (binary 0010, decimal 2)
```

Code Example Explanation

- **Shifts Right by 2**: The result, 0b0010, is 2 in decimal.

Notes

- Commonly used for dividing by powers of 2.
- Shifting right by 1 divides the number by 2.

Project: LED Pattern Control Using Bitwise Operations

Create a program that generates different LED patterns based on bitwise operations. The pattern will shift LEDs on and off using left and right shifts and allow control over which bits (LEDs) are active.

Project Circuit

Component	STM32 Pin	Connection Details
LEDs	D2-D5	Connect LEDs to pins D2, D3, D4, and D5 with resistors to GND

Project Code

```
from machine import Pin
import time

# Initialize LEDs on pins D2-D5
led_pins = [Pin("D2", Pin.OUT), Pin("D3", Pin.OUT), Pin("D4", Pin.OUT),
Pin("D5", Pin.OUT)]
# Function to display a binary pattern on LEDs
def display_pattern(pattern):
    for i in range(4):
        led_pins[i].value((pattern >> i) & 1)  # Set LED based on
shifted bit
# Main loop to create LED patterns
pattern = 0b0001  # Start with first LED on
while True:
    display_pattern(pattern)
    time.sleep(0.5)  # Wait to see the pattern
    # Shift pattern left, wrap around to create a looping effect
    pattern = (pattern << 1) & 0b1111  # Keep only the 4 bits
    if pattern == 0:
        pattern = 0b0001  # Reset pattern to start again
```

Save and Run

1. Save this code as main.py on your STM32 NUCLEO.
2. Run the script; the LEDs will light up in a shifting pattern, looping from one end to the other.

Check Output

The LEDs connected to pins D2-D5 will sequentially light up, shifting from one end to the other. This pattern demonstrates the use of bitwise shifts to control hardware.

Math Operations in STM32

Chapter Overview

Mathematical functions and constants are essential for embedded programming, allowing for data processing, calculations, and control of devices. MicroPython's `math` module includes a set of common mathematical operations such as square roots, powers, logarithms, trigonometric functions, and constants like π (pi) and e. This chapter covers each math function available in MicroPython, with syntax, detailed explanations, examples, and a practical project to demonstrate these concepts.

Chapter Goal

- Gain a solid understanding of mathematical functions in the MicroPython `math` module.
- Learn to apply various math operations for data processing and calculations.
- Implement a practical project that uses math operations to analyze sensor data in real time.

Rules

- **Import the Math Module**: Use `import math` to access MicroPython's math functions.
- **Use Constants for Accurate Calculations**: Constants like `math.pi` and `math.e` ensure precision in calculations.
- **Apply Functions Based on Input Requirements**: Use functions such as `sqrt` for roots and `sin` for trigonometric calculations.
- **Handle Negative Values Carefully**: Functions like `sqrt` and `log` require positive inputs.
- **Use Floating-Point Numbers for Precise Calculations**: Ensure correct types to avoid integer truncation in division and other operations.

Syntax Table

Serial No	Topic	Code Snippet	Simple Example
1	Square Root (`sqrt`)	`result = math.sqrt(x)`	`root = math.sqrt(16)`
2	Power (`pow`)	`result = math.pow(x, y)`	`cube = math.pow(2, 3)`
3	Exponential (`exp`)	`result = math.exp(x)`	`exp_val = math.exp(2)`
4	Natural Logarithm (`log`)	`result = math.log(x)`	`ln_val = math.log(10)`
5	Trigonometric Sine (`sin`)	`result = math.sin(x)`	`sine_val = math.sin(math.pi / 2)`
6	Trigonometric Cosine (`cos`)	`result = math.cos(x)`	`cos_val = math.cos(0)`
7	Trigonometric Tangent (`tan`)	`result = math.tan(x)`	`tan_val = math.tan(math.pi / 4)`
8	Constant pi	`math.pi`	`circumference = 2 * math.pi * radius`
9	Constant e	`math.e`	`growth = initial * math.e ** rate`

Topic Explanations

1. Square Root (sqrt)

What is Square Root?

The sqrt function computes the square root of a number, returning the value that, when multiplied by itself, gives the input number.

Use Purpose

- **Calculate Roots**: Used when square roots are needed, such as in geometric calculations.
- **Optimize Code**: Avoids using **0.5 or manual multiplication for square roots.

Syntax

```
result = math.sqrt(x)
```

Syntax Explanation

- **math.sqrt()**: This function is part of the math module, so the math module must be imported first.
- **x**: Represents the number whose square root you want to calculate. This must be a non-negative number for the function to work.
- **result**: Stores the square root of x as a floating-point number.

Simple Code Example

```
import math
value = 16
root = math.sqrt(value)  # Result is 4.0
```

Code Example Explanation

- **Calculates Square Root of 16**: The result, 4.0, is stored in root.

Notes

- Always returns a floating-point number.

- Input should be non-negative; passing a negative number will raise an error.

2. Power (pow)

What is Power?

The pow function raises a number to a specified exponent, equivalent to x**y.

Use Purpose

- **Exponentiation**: Calculates squares, cubes, and other powers.
- **Simplify Calculations**: Avoids repetitive multiplication.

Syntax

```
result = math.pow(x, y)
```

Syntax Explanation

- **math.pow()**: This function calculates the power of a number, requiring two arguments.
- **x**: Represents the base, or the number you want to raise.
- **y**: Represents the exponent, the power to which x will be raised.
- **result**: Stores the result of raising x to the power of y as a floating-point number.

Simple Code Example

```
import math
value = 2
power_val = math.pow(value, 3)   # Result is 8.0
```

Code Example Explanation

- **Calculates 2 Raised to the Power of 3**: The result, 8.0, is stored in power_val.

Notes

- Returns a float, even for integer powers.
- Can be used with fractional exponents for roots.

3. Exponential (exp)

What is Exponential?

The exp function computes e raised to the power of x, where e is the base of the natural logarithm (approximately 2.71828).

Use Purpose

- **Growth Calculations**: Commonly used in physics, biology, and financial applications.
- **Evaluate Exponential Functions**: Useful for exponential growth and decay.

Syntax

```
result = math.exp(x)
```

Syntax Explanation

- **math.exp()**: Part of the math module, calculates the power of e, the base of natural logarithms.
- **x**: Represents the exponent for e in the expression e^x.
- **result**: Stores the value of e raised to the power of x as a floating-point number.

Simple Code Example

```
import math
value = 2
exp_val = math.exp(value)  # Result is approximately 7.389
```

Code Example Explanation

- **Calculates e Raised to the Power of 2**: The result, approximately 7.389, is stored in exp_val.

Notes

- Commonly used in scientific calculations involving exponential growth.
- Large exponents may cause overflow.

Warnings

- Handle large inputs carefully to avoid overflow.

4. Natural Logarithm (log)

What is Natural Logarithm?

The log function computes the natural logarithm (base e) of a number, effectively reversing the exp function.

Use Purpose

- **Logarithmic Calculations**: Used in data transformations, scientific applications, and exponential growth models.
- **Reverses Exponentials**: Finds exponents for e-based growth models.

Syntax

```
result = math.log(x)
```

Syntax Explanation

- **math.log()**: Part of the math module, calculates the natural logarithm of a positive number.
- **x**: Represents the positive input value for which you want the natural logarithm.
- **result**: Stores the natural logarithm of x as a floating-point number.

Simple Code Example

```
import math
value = 10
ln_val = math.log(value)  # Result is approximately 2.302
```

Code Example Explanation

- **Calculates Natural Logarithm of 10**: Result, 2.302, is stored in ln_val.

Notes

- Works only with positive values.
- Commonly used in scientific data processing.

5. Trigonometric Sine (sin)

What is Trigonometric Sine?

The sin function calculates the sine of an angle in radians. It's widely used in wave-based applications, such as sound and signal processing.

Use Purpose

- **Calculate Wave Patterns**: Used in physics, signal processing, and oscillations.
- **Trigonometric Calculations**: Essential for geometric and rotational calculations.

Syntax

```
result = math.sin(x)
```

Syntax Explanation

- **math.sin()**: Calculates the sine of an angle expressed in radians.
- **x**: Represents the angle in radians for which you want the sine value.
- **result**: Stores the sine of x as a floating-point number.

Simple Code Example

```
import math
angle = math.pi / 2
sine_val = math.sin(angle)   # Result is 1.0
```

Code Example Explanation

- **Calculates Sine of 90 Degrees**: The result, 1.0, is stored in sine_val.

Notes

- Input should be in radians.
- Converts angles to radians using math.radians() if needed.

6. Trigonometric Cosine (cos)

What is Trigonometric Cosine?

The cos function calculates the cosine of an angle in radians, commonly used alongside the sine function.

Use Purpose

- **Trigonometric Calculations**: Useful for geometry, wave patterns, and oscillatory systems.
- **Periodic Calculations**: Commonly used in rotations and oscillations.

Syntax

```
result = math.cos(x)
```

Syntax Explanation

- **math.cos()**: Calculates the cosine of an angle expressed in radians.
- **x**: Represents the angle in radians for which you want the cosine value.
- **result**: Stores the cosine of x as a floating-point number.

Simple Code Example

```
import math
angle = 0
cos_val = math.cos(angle)  # Result is 1.0
```

Code Example Explanation

- **Calculates Cosine of 0 Degrees**: Result, 1.0, is stored in cos_val.

Notes

- Input should be in radians.
- Often used with the sine function.

Warnings

- Convert degrees to radians if necessary.

7. Trigonometric Tangent (tan)

What is Trigonometric Tangent?

The tan function calculates the tangent of an angle in radians, useful for slope and angle calculations in geometry.

Use Purpose

- **Calculate Ratios**: Useful in geometry and trigonometry.
- **Trigonometric Calculations**: Essential for analyzing slopes, angles, and wave patterns.

Syntax

```
result = math.tan(x)
```

Syntax Explanation

- **math.tan( )**: Calculates the tangent of an angle in radians.
- **x**: Represents the angle in radians for which you want the tangent value.
- **result**: Stores the tangent of x as a floating-point number.

Simple Code Example

```
import math
angle = math.pi / 4
tan_val = math.tan(angle)   # Result is approximately 1.0
```

Code Example Explanation

- **Calculates Tangent of 45 Degrees**: The result, 1.0, is stored in tan_val.

Notes

- Input should be in radians.
- Used for calculating slopes and angles.

Warnings

- Avoid using angles where tangent is undefined (e.g., π/2).

8. Constant pi

What is pi?

The constant `pi` represents the mathematical constant π (3.14159), commonly used in trigonometry, geometry, and wave calculations.

Use Purpose

- **Circle Calculations**: Used in formulas for circumference and area of circles.
- **Define Periods in Wave Functions**: Important for periodic calculations.

Syntax

```
math.pi
```

Simple Code Example

```
import math
radius = 5
circumference = 2 * math.pi * radius   # Result is approximately 31.4159
```

Code Example Explanation

- **Calculates Circle Circumference**: Uses `math.pi` for precision.

Notes

- Use `math.pi` for accurate circle and periodic calculations.

---

9. Constant e

What is e?

The constant e represents the base of the natural logarithm, approximately 2.71828. It is often used in exponential growth models and logarithmic calculations.

Use Purpose

- **Exponential Growth Models**: Widely used in finance, biology, and physics.
- **Evaluate e-based Expressions**: Forms the base for natural logarithmic functions.

Syntax

```
math.e
```

Simple Code Example

```
import math
rate = 0.05
growth = math.e ** rate  # Result is approximately 1.05127
```

Code Example Explanation

- **Calculates Exponential Growth**: Uses math.e for precise growth calculations.

Notes

- Use math.e in scientific and financial exponential expressions.

Final Project: Real-Time Sensor Data Analysis with Math Functions

Create a program that reads sensor values, performs mathematical calculations (square root, logarithm, and sine), and displays the results in real-time.

Project Circuit

Component	STM32 Pin	Connection Details
Potentiometer	A1	Connect one end to 3.3V, the other to GND, and wiper to A1

Project Code

```python
from machine import ADC, Pin
import math
import time

# Initialize potentiometer on ADC pin A1
sensor = ADC(Pin("A1"))

while True:
    # Read sensor value
    sensor_value = sensor.read_u16()

    # Calculate square root, natural log, and sine of the sensor value
    root = math.sqrt(sensor_value)
    log_value = math.log(sensor_value + 1)  # Adding 1 to avoid log(0)
    sine_value = math.sin(sensor_value * math.pi / 65535)  # Scale to
0-π

    # Display calculated values
    print(f"Sensor Value: {sensor_value}, Sqrt: {root:.2f}, Log:
{log_value:.2f}, Sin: {sine_value:.2f}")

    # Delay for readability
    time.sleep(1)
```

Save and Run

1. Save this code as main.py on your STM32 NUCLEO.
2. Run the script; adjusting the potentiometer will generate real-time calculations of the square root, logarithm, and sine of the sensor value.

Check Output

As the potentiometer value changes, the code outputs the sensor reading along with calculated square root, logarithmic, and sine values in real time.

Character Manipulation in STM32

Chapter Overview

Character manipulation is essential in embedded systems for handling text data, working with user inputs, formatting outputs, and generating responses. MicroPython provides several functions and methods to work with individual characters, enabling conversions, formatting, and checking properties like alphanumeric status or case. This chapter covers the most useful character operations in MicroPython, with syntax, explanations, examples, and a practical project.

Chapter Goal

- Understand and use character manipulation functions in MicroPython.
- Learn how to handle individual characters and character-related operations.
- Implement a practical project to read and display characters based on sensor input or user-defined conditions.

Rules

- **Use String Functions for Character Manipulation**: Use functions like ord(), chr(), isalpha(), isdigit() for character handling.
- **Handle Upper and Lowercase Carefully**: Use upper() and lower() to standardize case as needed.
- **Validate Characters for Input Control**: Check properties of characters (e.g., is it a digit or letter) to ensure valid inputs.
- **Use ASCII Conversions**: Use ord() and chr() to convert between characters and their ASCII values.
- **Be Mindful of Unicode in Text Processing**: Only use ASCII characters if the embedded system doesn't support extended Unicode.

Syntax Table

Serial No	Topic	Code Snippet	Simple Example
1	Convert Character to ASCII (ord)	`ascii_value = ord(character)`	`ascii_val = ord('A')`
2	Convert ASCII to Character (chr)	`character = chr(ascii_value)`	`char = chr(65)`
3	Check if Alphabetic (isalpha)	`is_alpha = character.isalpha()`	`'A'.isalpha()`
4	Check if Digit (isdigit)	`is_digit = character.isdigit()`	`'5'.isdigit()`
5	Convert to Uppercase (upper)	`uppercase = character.upper()`	`'a'.upper()`
6	Convert to Lowercase (lower)	`lowercase = character.lower()`	`'A'.lower()`
7	Check if Alphanumeric (isalnum)	`is_alnum = character.isalnum()`	`'A5'.isalnum()`
8	Strip Whitespaces (strip)	`stripped = string.strip()`	`' text '.strip()`

Topic Explanations

1. Convert Character to ASCII (ord)

What is ord?

The ord function converts a single character to its corresponding ASCII (or Unicode) integer value.

Use Purpose

- **ASCII Conversion**: Used to find the ASCII value of a character for encoding or protocol processing.
- **Data Analysis**: Useful when checking or manipulating characters based on their ASCII values.

Syntax

```
ascii_value = ord(character)
```

Syntax Explanation

- **ord( )**: The function that takes a single character as input.
- **character**: A single character (string of length 1) whose ASCII value is desired.
- **ascii_value**: Stores the integer ASCII value of character.

Simple Code Example

```
character = 'A'
ascii_value = ord(character)  # Result is 65
```

Code Example Explanation

- **Converts Character 'A' to ASCII**: The result, 65, is stored in ascii_value.

Notes

- Only works for single characters.
- Use in applications where character encoding is necessary.

2. Convert ASCII to Character (chr)

What is chr?

The chr function converts an ASCII (or Unicode) integer value to its corresponding character.

Use Purpose

- **ASCII to Character Conversion**: Useful when generating characters based on ASCII values.
- **Data Decoding**: Used in protocols where data needs to be displayed as characters.

Syntax

```
character = chr(ascii_value)
```

Syntax Explanation

- **chr()**: The function that takes an ASCII value as input.
- **ascii_value**: An integer representing an ASCII value (0-127).
- **character**: Stores the character corresponding to the ASCII value.

Simple Code Example

```
ascii_value = 65
character = chr(ascii_value)   # Result is 'A'
```

Code Example Explanation

- **Converts ASCII Value 65 to Character**: The result, 'A', is stored in character.

Notes

- Only works with integers within the valid ASCII range.
- Useful in data encoding and decoding.

Warnings

- Passing values outside the ASCII range raises a ValueError.

3. Check if Alphabetic (`isalpha`)

What is `isalpha`?

The `isalpha` method checks if a character (or string) consists only of alphabetic characters (A-Z or a-z).

Use Purpose

- **Validate Input**: Used to ensure only letters are included in a string or character.
- **Conditional Checks**: Useful in conditions where alphabetic characters are required.

Syntax

```
is_alpha = character.isalpha()
```

Syntax Explanation

- **`isalpha()`**: This method checks if a character or string contains only letters.
- **`character`**: A string whose characters you want to check.
- **`is_alpha`**: Boolean result, `True` if all characters are alphabetic, otherwise `False`.

Simple Code Example

```
character = 'A'
is_alpha = character.isalpha()  # Result is True
```

Code Example Explanation

- **Checks if Character 'A' is Alphabetic**: The result, `True`, is stored in `is_alpha`.

Notes

- Returns `True` for uppercase and lowercase letters only.
- Often used in input validation.

Warnings

- Returns `False` for empty strings.

4. Check if Digit (`isdigit`)

What is `isdigit`?

The `isdigit` method checks if a character (or string) consists only of digits (0-9).

Use Purpose

- **Validate Numeric Input**: Ensures only digits are in a string.
- **Conditional Checks**: Used in conditions requiring numeric characters.

Syntax

```
is_digit = character.isdigit()
```

Syntax Explanation

- **`isdigit()`**: This method checks if a string contains only numeric characters.
- **`character`**: A string you want to check for digit-only content.
- **`is_digit`**: Boolean result, True if all characters are digits, otherwise False.

Simple Code Example

```
character = '5'
is_digit = character.isdigit()   # Result is True
```

Code Example Explanation

- **Checks if Character '5' is a Digit**: The result, True, is stored in `is_digit`.

Notes

- Only returns True if all characters in the string are digits.
- Commonly used in numeric validation.

Warnings

- Returns False for empty strings.

5. Convert to Uppercase (upper)

What is upper?

The upper method converts a character or string to uppercase, if it is not already.

Use Purpose

- **Standardize Case**: Useful in applications requiring consistent case.
- **Prepare for Comparisons**: Converts text to uppercase to enable case-insensitive comparisons.

Syntax

```
uppercase = character.upper()
```

Syntax Explanation

- **upper()**: Converts all lowercase letters in a string to uppercase.
- **character**: A string you want to convert to uppercase.
- **uppercase**: Stores the converted uppercase string.

Simple Code Example

```
character = 'a'
uppercase = character.upper()   # Result is 'A'
```

Code Example Explanation

- **Converts 'a' to Uppercase**: The result, 'A', is stored in uppercase.

Notes

- Does not change non-alphabetic characters.
- Useful in case-insensitive applications.

Warnings

- Does not modify the original string; it returns a new one.

6. Convert to Lowercase (lower)

What is lower?

The lower method converts a character or string to lowercase, if it is not already.

Use Purpose

- **Standardize Case**: Useful for case consistency.
- **Prepare for Comparisons**: Converts text to lowercase for case-insensitive comparisons.

Syntax

```
lowercase = character.lower()
```

Syntax Explanation

- **lower()**: Converts all uppercase letters in a string to lowercase.
- **character**: A string you want to convert to lowercase.
- **lowercase**: Stores the converted lowercase string.

Simple Code Example

```
character = 'A'
lowercase = character.lower()  # Result is 'a'
```

Code Example Explanation

- **Converts 'A' to Lowercase**: The result, 'a', is stored in lowercase.

Notes

- Does not change non-alphabetic characters.
- Useful in case-insensitive applications.

Warnings

- Does not modify the original string; it returns a new one.

7. Check if Alphanumeric (`isalnum`)

What is `isalnum`?

The `isalnum` method checks if a character or string consists only of alphanumeric characters (letters and numbers).

Use Purpose

- **Validate Input**: Used in situations where letters and numbers are acceptable, but no special characters.
- **Conditional Checks**: Often used in ID or code validation.

Syntax

```
is_alnum = character.isalnum()
```

Syntax Explanation

- `isalnum()`: Checks if all characters in the string are either letters or digits.
- `character`: A string to check for alphanumeric content.
- `is_alnum`: Boolean result, `True` if all characters are alphanumeric, otherwise `False`.

Simple Code Example

```
character = 'A5'
is_alnum = character.isalnum()  # Result is True
```

Code Example Explanation

- **Checks if 'A5' is Alphanumeric**: The result, `True`, is stored in `is_alnum`.

Notes

- Returns `False` if there are any special characters.
- Useful for validating identifiers.

Warnings

- Returns `False` for empty strings.

8. Strip Whitespaces (`strip`)

What is `strip`?

The `strip` method removes leading and trailing whitespace from a string, which is useful for cleaning up user input.

Use Purpose

- **Remove Extra Spaces**: Used to clean up strings before processing or storing.
- **Prepare for Comparisons**: Ensures only actual content is compared by removing unnecessary spaces.

Syntax

```
stripped = string.strip()
```

Syntax Explanation

- `strip()`: Removes any leading and trailing spaces from a string.
- `string`: The string you want to clean.
- `stripped`: Stores the cleaned version of the string.

Simple Code Example

```
text = '   hello   '
stripped = text.strip()  # Result is 'hello'
```

Code Example Explanation

- **Removes Extra Spaces from 'hello'**: The result, `'hello'`, is stored in `stripped`.

Notes

- Does not remove spaces within the string, only at the start and end.
- Commonly used in input sanitization.

Warnings

- Returns the original string if no whitespace is present.

Final Project: Character-Based User Input Validation

Project Objective

Create a program that reads user input from a sensor (or simulated input) and validates it to ensure it only contains uppercase alphanumeric characters. If the input is valid, it will be displayed; otherwise, an error message will be shown.

Project Code

```python
import time

# Simulated user input function for demonstration
def read_user_input():
    # Replace this with actual user input or sensor data in a real
setup
    return 'A5C '

while True:
    user_input = read_user_input().strip()  # Clean the input
    is_valid = True

    # Validate each character in the input
    for char in user_input:
        if not char.isalnum() or not char.isupper():
            is_valid = False
            break

    # Display results
    if is_valid:
        print(f"Valid Input: {user_input}")
    else:
        print("Error: Input must be uppercase and alphanumeric.")

    # Wait before next iteration
    time.sleep(1)
```

Save and Run

1. Save this code as main.py on your STM32 NUCLEO.
2. Run the script; the program will read a simulated input, validate it, and display whether it meets the uppercase alphanumeric requirement.

Check Output

The console will display "Valid Input" if the input meets the criteria or an error message if it does not.

Random Number Generation in STM32

Chapter Overview

Random number generation is essential in embedded systems for tasks such as simulations, games, testing, and security. MicroPython's random module offers various functions for generating random numbers, choosing random elements, and shuffling sequences. This chapter covers the most useful random number functions in MicroPython, with syntax, explanations, examples, and a practical project.

Chapter Goal

- Understand and use random number generation functions in MicroPython.
- Learn to generate integers, floats, and use random choices or shuffles.
- Implement a practical project to simulate random behavior in an LED pattern generator.

Rules

- **Import the Random Module**: Use import random to access the random number functions.
- **Use Appropriate Functions Based on Data Type**: Choose between randint, random, and uniform based on the type of random value required.
- **Set Random Seed for Reproducibility**: Use seed() if you need reproducible random sequences.
- **Handle Floating-Point Operations Carefully**: Be mindful of rounding when using random floats in comparisons.
- **Avoid Using Random in Sensitive Security**: For high-security applications, use dedicated cryptographic random functions instead of random.

Syntax Table

Serial No	Topic	Code Snippet	Simple Example
1	Generate Random Integer (randint)	`rand_num = random.randint(a, b)`	`rand_int = random.randint(1, 10)`
2	Generate Random Float (random)	`rand_num = random.random()`	`rand_float = random.random()`
3	Generate Random Float in Range (uniform)	`rand_num = random.uniform(a, b)`	`rand_float = random.uniform(1.0, 5.0)`
4	Select Random Element (choice)	`rand_elem = random.choice(sequence)`	`rand_item = random.choice([1, 2, 3])`
5	Shuffle Sequence (shuffle)	`random.shuffle(sequence)`	`random.shuffle([1, 2, 3])`
6	Set Random Seed (seed)	`random.seed(value)`	`random.seed(10)`

Topic Explanations

1. Generate Random Integer (`randint`)

What is `randint`?

The `randint` function generates a random integer within a specified range, including both endpoints. This function is useful for generating discrete random values, such as selecting random items or steps.

Use Purpose

- **Random Selection in Ranges**: Used for generating random numbers within specific limits.
- **Discrete Random Choices**: Ideal for games, simulations, or other cases needing whole numbers.

Syntax

```
rand_num = random.randint(a, b)
```

Syntax Explanation

- **`random.randint()`**: Generates a random integer in the inclusive range [a, b].
- **a**: The start of the range (included).
- **b**: The end of the range (included).
- **`rand_num`**: Stores the generated random integer.

Simple Code Example

```
import random
rand_int = random.randint(1, 10)  # Result is a random integer from 1
to 10
```

Code Example Explanation

- **Generates Random Integer from 1 to 10**: A random integer is generated and stored in `rand_int`.

Notes

- Useful when random whole numbers are needed within specific bounds.
- Commonly used in loops or conditions for random selections.

2. Generate Random Float (`random`)

What is `random`?

The `random` function generates a random floating-point number between 0.0 and 1.0, excluding 1.0. It's helpful for probability-based decisions and scaling random values to custom ranges.

Use Purpose

- **Generate Probabilities**: Used in simulations requiring probability values between 0 and 1.
- **Scale to Custom Ranges**: Can be multiplied to create random floats within custom ranges.

Syntax

```
rand_num = random.random()
```

Syntax Explanation

- **`random.random()`**: Generates a random float in the range `[0.0, 1.0)`.
- **`rand_num`**: Stores the generated random float.

Simple Code Example

```
import random
rand_float = random.random()  # Result is a random float between 0.0
and 1.0
```

Code Example Explanation

- **Generates Random Float between 0.0 and 1.0**: The result is stored in `rand_float`.

Notes

- Multiply the result to achieve a custom range, e.g., `random.random() * 10` for 0 to 10.
- Useful for percentage-based conditions.

3. Generate Random Float in Range (`uniform`)

What is `uniform`?

The `uniform` function generates a random floating-point number within a specified range, including both endpoints. It provides greater flexibility compared to `random` by allowing custom ranges directly.

Use Purpose

- **Continuous Random Values in Ranges**: Ideal for generating random values between custom float limits.
- **Simulations and Randomization**: Useful for applications needing precise random floats.

Syntax

```
rand_num = random.uniform(a, b)
```

Syntax Explanation

- **`random.uniform()`**: Generates a random float in the inclusive range [a, b].
- **a**: The start of the range.
- **b**: The end of the range.
- **`rand_num`**: Stores the generated random float.

Simple Code Example

```
import random
rand_float = random.uniform(1.0, 5.0)  # Result is a random float
between 1.0 and 5.0
```

Code Example Explanation

- **Generates Random Float between 1.0 and 5.0**: The result is stored in `rand_float`.

Notes

- Allows direct specification of any float range.
- Commonly used in simulations and games.

4. Select Random Element (choice)

What is choice?

The choice function selects a random element from a sequence, such as a list or tuple. It's useful for randomly picking from predefined options.

Use Purpose

- **Random Selection from Lists**: Useful in scenarios where you need to pick a random item from a predefined list.
- **Simulating Random Events**: Ideal for games, quizzes, or situations requiring random choices.

Syntax

```
rand_elem = random.choice(sequence)
```

Syntax Explanation

- **random.choice()**: Chooses a random item from a given sequence.
- **sequence**: The list or tuple from which to select a random element.
- **rand_elem**: Stores the randomly selected element.

Simple Code Example

```
import random
rand_item = random.choice([1, 2, 3])  # Result is a random choice from
the list [1, 2, 3]
```

Code Example Explanation

- **Randomly Selects an Item from List**: The randomly chosen item is stored in rand_item.

Notes

- Works with any sequence type, including lists, tuples, and strings.
- Often used to randomly choose predefined options.

5. Shuffle Sequence (shuffle)

What is shuffle?

The shuffle function randomly shuffles the elements in a sequence in place, altering the order of elements each time it's called.

Use Purpose

- **Randomize Order**: Used to randomize elements in lists for games, tests, or simulations.
- **Create Randomized Sequences**: Ideal for shuffling a sequence to ensure random order.

Syntax

```
random.shuffle(sequence)
```

Syntax Explanation

- **random.shuffle()**: Shuffles a sequence (list) in place, changing the order of elements.
- **sequence**: A list to shuffle. This list is modified in place.

Simple Code Example

```
import random
items = [1, 2, 3]
random.shuffle(items)  # Modifies `items` to be in random order, e.g.,
[2, 1, 3]
```

Code Example Explanation

- **Shuffles Items in the List**: The original list items is modified to a random order.

Notes

- Only works on mutable sequences (e.g., lists).
- Useful for shuffling card decks, questions, or item orders.

Warnings

- Does not return a new list; modifies the existing list.

6. Set Random Seed (seed)

What is seed?

The seed function initializes the random number generator to a fixed state, allowing for reproducible random sequences. This is particularly useful for testing.

Use Purpose

- **Reproduce Random Sequences**: Ensures the same random sequence for debugging or testing.
- **Control Randomness**: Sets a predictable random sequence when using a fixed seed value.

Syntax

```
random.seed(value)
```

Syntax Explanation

- **random.seed()**: Sets the seed value for the random number generator.
- **value**: An integer seed to initialize the random generator. Same seed produces the same sequence.

Simple Code Example

```
import random
random.seed(10)   # Sets the seed to 10, producing a predictable
sequence
```

Code Example Explanation

- **Sets Seed for Reproducibility**: Using seed 10 ensures the same sequence every time.

Notes

- Use seed() with a specific value to reproduce results.
- Useful for testing and debugging.

Final Project: Random LED Blinker

Project Objective

Create a program that randomly turns an LED on and off at varying intervals, using random functions to generate random delays and random states.

Project Circuit

Component	STM32 Pin	Connection Details
LED	D2	Connect LED to pin D2 with a resistor to GND

Project Code

```python
from machine import Pin
import random
import time

# Initialize LED on pin D2
led = Pin("D2", Pin.OUT)

# Main loop to blink LED with random intervals and random states
while True:
    # Set LED state to ON or OFF randomly
    led.value(random.choice([0, 1]))
    # Wait for a random delay between 0.1 and 1.0 seconds
    delay = random.uniform(0.1, 1.0)
    print(f"LED state: {led.value()}, Delay: {delay:.2f} seconds")

    # Wait for the random delay
    time.sleep(delay)
```

Save and Run

1. Save this code as main.py on your STM32 NUCLEO.
2. Run the script; the LED will blink randomly, with varying delays and states.

Check Output

The LED on pin D2 will turn on and off at random intervals, simulating unpredictable behavior based on random values.

Communication Protocols in STM32

Chapter Overview

Communication protocols enable embedded systems to communicate with each other or with peripherals, such as sensors, displays, and computers. STM32 supports common protocols like UART, I2C, and SPI, each suited for specific purposes. MicroPython offers support for these protocols, making it easier to interface with various devices. This chapter covers each protocol in detail, with syntax, examples, and a practical project to demonstrate communication between devices.

Chapter Goal

- Understand the basics of UART, I2C, and SPI protocols and how to implement them in MicroPython.
- Learn how to send and receive data between STM32 and external devices.
- Implement a practical project using I2C to communicate with an external sensor and display data.

Rules

- **Initialize Communication Properly**: Ensure correct initialization for each protocol to avoid communication errors.
- **Use Appropriate Protocol for Device Type**: UART for simple serial communication, I2C for multi-device setups, and SPI for high-speed devices.
- **Handle Errors Gracefully**: Implement error-handling to manage communication issues, such as missing devices or incorrect configurations.
- **Terminate Communication**: Properly close or reset communication in some protocols after data transfer.
- **Check Data Availability Before Reading**: Always verify data is available to avoid reading errors.

Syntax Table

Serial No	Protocol	Code Snippet	Simple Example
1	UART Initialize	`uart = UART(port, baudrate)`	`uart = UART(1, 9600)`
2	UART Send Data	`uart.write(data)`	`uart.write(b'Hello')`
3	UART Read Data	`data = uart.read(size)`	`data = uart.read(5)`
4	I2C Initialize	`i2c = I2C(port, freq=freq)`	`i2c = I2C(1, freq=400000)`
5	I2C Scan	`devices = i2c.scan()`	`devices = i2c.scan()`
6	I2C Read Data	`data = i2c.readfrom(addr, size)`	`data = i2c.readfrom(0x3C, 4)`
7	I2C Write Data	`i2c.writeto(addr, data)`	`i2c.writeto(0x3C, b'\x00\x01')`

8	SPI Initialize	`spi = SPI(port, baudrate=baudrate)`	`spi = SPI(1, baudrate=100000 0)`
9	SPI Send Data	`spi.write(data)`	`spi.write(b'\x AA\xBB')`
10	SPI Read Data	`data = spi.read(size)`	`data = spi.read(2)`

Topic Explanations

1. UART (Universal Asynchronous Receiver/Transmitter)

What is UART?

UART is a simple, asynchronous, serial communication protocol that sends and receives data byte-by-byte between two devices. It's often used to communicate with PCs, microcontrollers, and GPS modules.

Use Purpose

- **Simple Data Transfer**: Used for transmitting and receiving data without a clock signal.
- **Two-Way Communication**: Allows bidirectional data transfer with minimal wiring (TX and RX pins).

Syntax

```
uart = UART(port, baudrate)
uart.write(data)
data = uart.read(size)
```

Syntax Explanation

- **UART(port, baudrate)**: Initializes the UART on a specific port with a given baudrate.
- **port**: UART port number (e.g., 1).

- **baudrate**: Communication speed in bits per second (e.g., 9600, 115200).
- **write(data)**: Sends data as bytes to the connected device.
- **read(size)**: Reads size bytes of data received over UART.

Simple Code Example

```python
from machine import UART

# Initialize UART1 with a baud rate of 9600
uart = UART(1, 9600)

# Send data
uart.write(b'Hello')

# Read data if available
if uart.any():
    received_data = uart.read(5)
    print(received_data)
```

Code Example Explanation
- **Initializes UART1 at 9600 Baud**: Configures UART1 to communicate at 9600 bps.
- **Sends and Receives Data**: Sends "Hello" and reads 5 bytes if data is available.

Notes
- Requires TX and RX connections between devices.
- Commonly used for console debugging and communication with serial peripherals.

Warnings
- Ensure matching baud rates on both devices for reliable communication.

---

2. I2C (Inter-Integrated Circuit)

What is I2C?
I2C is a synchronous, multi-master, multi-slave communication protocol that allows multiple devices to connect using only two wires:

SDA (data line) and SCL (clock line). Each device has a unique address.

Use Purpose

- **Multi-Device Communication**: Supports multiple devices on the same bus.
- **Efficient and Scalable**: Ideal for connecting sensors, displays, and memory.

Syntax

```
i2c = I2C(port, freq=freq)
devices = i2c.scan()
data = i2c.readfrom(addr, size)
i2c.writeto(addr, data)
```

Syntax Explanation

- **I2C(port, freq=freq)**: Initializes the I2C communication on a specific port and frequency.
- **port**: I2C port number (e.g., 1).
- **freq**: I2C bus speed in Hertz (e.g., 400000 for 400 kHz).
- **scan()**: Detects devices connected to the I2C bus, returning their addresses.
- **readfrom(addr, size)**: Reads size bytes from the device at address addr.
- **writeto(addr, data)**: Sends data to the device at address addr.

Simple Code Example

```
from machine import I2C

# Initialize I2C on port 1 with a frequency of 400 kHz
i2c = I2C(1, freq=400000)

# Scan for devices on the I2C bus
devices = i2c.scan()
print("I2C Devices:", devices)

# Read 4 bytes from a device at address 0x3C
data = i2c.readfrom(0x3C, 4)
print("Data:", data)

# Write data to the device
i2c.writeto(0x3C, b'\x00\x01')
```

Code Example Explanation

- **Initializes I2C at 400 kHz**: Configures I2C on port 1 for high-speed communication.
- **Scans and Interacts with I2C Device**: Detects connected devices, reads, and writes data to address 0x3C.

Notes
- Each device must have a unique address.
- I2C is suitable for low to moderate-speed communication.

---

3. SPI (Serial Peripheral Interface)

What is SPI?
SPI is a high-speed, synchronous, serial communication protocol commonly used for short-distance communication between a microcontroller and peripherals like sensors, displays, and memory modules.

Use Purpose
- **High-Speed Data Transfer**: Suitable for devices requiring fast communication.
- **Multiple Devices**: Supports multiple devices using individual Chip Select (CS) lines.

Syntax
```
spi = SPI(port, baudrate=baudrate)
spi.write(data)
data = spi.read(size)
```

Syntax Explanation
- `SPI(port, baudrate=baudrate)`: Initializes the SPI communication on a specific port and baudrate.
- `port`: SPI port number (e.g., 1).
- `baudrate`: SPI clock speed in bits per second.
- `write(data)`: Sends data as bytes over SPI.
- `read(size)`: Reads size bytes from the SPI bus.

Simple Code Example

```
from machine import SPI

# Initialize SPI on port 1 with a baud rate of 1 MHz
spi = SPI(1, baudrate=1000000)

# Send data
spi.write(b'\xAA\xBB')

# Read 2 bytes of data
received_data = spi.read(2)
print("Received:", received_data)
```

Code Example Explanation

- **Initializes SPI at 1 MHz**: Configures SPI on port 1 with a 1 MHz clock.
- **Sends and Receives Data**: Transmits two bytes and reads two bytes.

Notes

- Requires three connections: MISO, MOSI, and SCK.
- Multiple devices can be added using individual CS lines.

Warnings

- Ensure proper clock polarity and phase configuration for each device.

Final Project: Temperature Sensor Reading via I2C

Create a program that reads temperature data from an I2C-based temperature sensor (e.g., TMP102 or similar) and displays it on the console. The program will initialize the I2C bus, scan for devices, and communicate with the sensor to obtain and display the temperature.

Project Circuit

Component	STM32 Pin	Connection Details

Temperature Sensor	SDA	Connect to SDA pin on STM32
	SCL	Connect to SCL pin on STM32
	VCC	Connect to 3.3V
	GND	Connect to GND

Project Code

```python
from machine import I2C, Pin
import time

# Initialize I2C on port 1 with 400 kHz
i2c = I2C(1, freq=400000)

# Function to read temperature from the sensor
def read_temperature(addr):
    # Read two bytes of data from the sensor
    data = i2c.readfrom(addr, 2)
    # Convert to temperature (assuming 12-bit resolution, TMP102
format)
    temp = ((data[0] << 4) | (data[1] >> 4)) * 0.0625
    return temp

# Scan I2C bus for devices
devices = i2c.scan()
if devices:
    print("I2C Devices Found:", devices)
    temp_sensor_addr = devices[0]  # Use the first found device as the
temperature sensor
else:
    print("No I2C devices found.")
    temp_sensor_addr = None

# Main loop to read temperature
while temp_sensor_addr is not None:
    temperature = read_temperature(temp_sensor_addr)
    print("Temperature:", temperature, "°C")
    time.sleep(1)  # Delay for readability
```

Save and Run

1. Save this code as main.py on your STM32 NUCLEO.

2. Run the script; the program will scan for I2C devices, detect the temperature sensor, and continuously read and display the temperature.

Check Output

The console will display the temperature readings from the sensor in real time, updating every second.

Print Statements in STM32

Chapter Overview

The `print` function is essential in embedded programming for debugging, displaying data, and providing real-time feedback. In MicroPython, `print` can display strings, numbers, and formatted data in the console. This chapter covers various ways to use `print` in MicroPython, with syntax, formatting options, examples, and a practical project.

Chapter Goal

- Understand the basics of using `print` statements in MicroPython.
- Learn to format and display different data types with `print`.
- Implement a practical project using `print` to display sensor readings in a formatted manner.

Rules

- **Use `print` for Debugging and Data Display**: Leverage `print` to check variable values and display program progress.

- **Format Strings for Clarity**: Use formatting options to make output clear and easy to read.
- **Combine Data Types in Output**: Use f-strings or `format()` to combine strings with other data types.
- **Limit Print Frequency in Loops**: Minimize excessive prints in tight loops to avoid slowing down the program.
- **Use Escape Characters for Formatting**: Use \n for newlines and \t for tabs to structure the output.

Syntax Table

Serial No	Topic	Code Snippet	Simple Example
1	Basic Print	`print(value)`	`print("Hello")`
2	Print Multiple Values	`print(value1, value2, ...)`	`print("Temp:", 25)`
3	Print with Separator	`print(value1, value2, sep="separator")`	`print("Hello", "World", sep="-")`
4	Print with End	`print(value, end="end_character")`	`print("Loading", end="...")`
5	Print Formatted String (%)	`print("format" % values)`	`print("Temp: %d C" % temp)`

6	Print with format()	`print("{}".format(value))`	`print("Temp: {} C".format(temp))`
7	Print with f-strings	`print(f"text {value}")`	`print(f"Temp: {temp} C")`
8	Escape Characters	`\n, \t, \\`	`print("Hello\n World")`

Topic Explanations

1. Basic Print

What is Basic Print?

The `print` function outputs a specified value or variable to the console. It is commonly used to display text or data, making it essential for debugging and providing real-time feedback in embedded systems.

Use Purpose

- **Display Messages**: Used to display simple text or messages.
- **Debugging**: Helps check variable values and program flow.

Syntax

```
print(value)
```

Syntax Explanation

- **print()**: The function that outputs text or variable values to the console.
- **value**: The value or text to print.

Simple Code Example

```
print("Hello, World!")
```

Code Example Explanation

- **Outputs "Hello, World!" to Console**: The text inside the quotation marks is displayed as-is.

Notes

- Can print any data type (e.g., strings, numbers).
- Outputs a newline at the end by default.

Warnings

- Ensure proper data type compatibility when printing non-string values.

---

2. Print Multiple Values

What is Print Multiple Values?

The print function can output multiple values separated by commas, displaying them in sequence with spaces by default.

Use Purpose

- **Combine Data**: Allows combining text and variable values in a single print statement.
- **Display Multiple Outputs**: Useful for outputting multiple pieces of information in one line.

Syntax

```
print(value1, value2, ...)
```

Syntax Explanation

- **print()**: Outputs the specified values.
- **value1, value2, ...**: Multiple values separated by commas. Each value is printed with a space in between.

Simple Code Example

```
temp = 25
```

```
print("Temperature:", temp)
```

Code Example Explanation

- **Prints "Temperature: 25" to Console**: Displays text and the temp variable value.

Notes

- Automatically adds a space between values.
- Useful for combining text and data without additional formatting.

Warnings

- Non-string data will be converted to a string for display.

---

3. Print with Separator

What is Print with Separator?

The print function's sep argument specifies a custom separator to use between multiple values, instead of the default space.

Use Purpose

- **Custom Separators**: Ideal for formatted output where specific delimiters are required, like commas or hyphens.
- **Improve Readability**: Adds clarity when printing lists or data items.

Syntax

```
print(value1, value2, sep="separator")
```

Syntax Explanation

- **sep**: Optional argument defining the separator between values.
- **"separator"**: Specifies the separator string (e.g., "-" or ",").

Simple Code Example

```
print("Hello", "World", sep="-")
```

Code Example Explanation
- **Prints "Hello-World"**: Uses a hyphen instead of a space to separate the words.

Notes
- The separator applies between all values in the print statement.
- Often used to structure output data with delimiters.

Warnings
- Using sep without multiple values has no effect.

---

4. Print with End

What is Print with End?
The print function's end argument defines what to print at the end of the output, instead of the default newline.

Use Purpose
- **Modify Line Endings**: Useful for printing multiple outputs on the same line.
- **Control Formatting**: Provides flexibility in how output lines are terminated.

Syntax
```
print(value, end="end_character")
```

Syntax Explanation
- **end**: Optional argument specifying the character to print at the end.
- **"end_character"**: Custom end character, such as an ellipsis (" . . . ").

Simple Code Example

```
print("Loading", end="...")
```

Code Example Explanation

- **Prints "Loading..."**: Replaces the default newline with three dots.

Notes

- Commonly used in progress indicators.
- The next print statement will continue on the same line if end is not set to newline.

Warnings

- Using end incorrectly may result in unexpected formatting.

---

5. Print Formatted String (%)

What is Print Formatted String (%)?

The % operator allows formatting strings by embedding variables within a specified format.

Use Purpose

- **Embed Variables in Text**: Useful for formatting output with variables in specific formats.
- **Display Numeric Precision**: Control the precision of numeric output.

Syntax

```
print("format" % values)
```

Syntax Explanation

- **"format" % values**: Format string containing placeholders (%d for integers, %f for floats, etc.).
- **values**: Values corresponding to each placeholder.

Simple Code Example

```
temp = 25
```

```
print("Temperature: %d C" % temp)
```

Code Example Explanation

- **Prints "Temperature: 25 C"**: Inserts the value of `temp` into the formatted string.

Notes

- Supports %d for integers, %f for floats, %s for strings.
- Useful for controlling numeric precision with %.2f for two decimal places.

Warnings

- Ensure format specifiers match the data type of variables.

---

6. Print with `format()`

What is Print with `format()`?

The `format()` method allows embedding variables in a string using placeholders `{}`, which are replaced with values passed to `format()`.

Use Purpose

- **Flexible String Formatting**: Useful for creating complex formatted strings.
- **Embed Multiple Values**: Works well for displaying multiple variables.

Syntax

```
print("{}".format(value))
```

Syntax Explanation

- `"{}".format(value)`: Uses `{}` as placeholders in the string, replaced with values provided in `format()`.

Simple Code Example

```
temp = 25
print("Temperature: {} C".format(temp))
```

Code Example Explanation

- **Prints "Temperature: 25 C"**: Inserts the value of `temp` into the string.

Notes

- Allows multiple placeholders (e.g., `"{} and {}".format(val1, val2)`).
- Useful for aligning text or numbers.

Warnings

- Ensure correct order and number of placeholders for the values.

---

7. Print with f-strings

What is Print with f-strings?

An f-string is a formatted string literal that embeds variables directly in a string using curly braces {} and a leading f.

Use Purpose

- **Concise String Formatting**: Combines readability with flexibility.
- **Embed Expressions**: Supports inline expressions for calculations within the string.

Syntax

```
print(f"text {value}")
```

Syntax Explanation

- **f"text {value}"**: The f before the string allows embedding variables within {} directly in the string.

Simple Code Example

```
temp = 25
```

```
print(f"Temperature: {temp} C")
```

Code Example Explanation

- **Prints "Temperature: 25 C"**: Embeds temp directly in the string.

Notes

- Allows embedding calculations directly, like f"Result: {a + b}".
- Great for clean, readable formatting.

Warnings

- Only available in Python 3.6+ (included in MicroPython).

---

8. Escape Characters

What are Escape Characters?

Escape characters are special sequences in strings that represent whitespace, newlines, tabs, or special symbols.

Use Purpose

- **Format Output**: Allows multi-line strings or tabbed layouts.
- **Insert Special Characters**: Enables displaying special characters, such as quotation marks or backslashes.

Syntax

- **\n**: Newline
- **\t**: Tab
- ****: Backslash

Syntax Explanation

- **\n**: Moves to the next line.
- **\t**: Adds a tab space.
- ****: Prints a backslash character.

Simple Code Example

```python
print("Hello\nWorld")
print("Item\tPrice")
print("Backslash: \\")
```

Code Example Explanation

- **Prints "Hello" on One Line and "World" on the Next**: Uses newline escape.
- **Prints "Item" and "Price" with Tab Space**: Uses tab escape.

Notes

- Commonly used for organizing output into readable blocks.
- Essential for formatted console displays.

Warnings

- Use escape characters correctly to avoid unintended results.

Final Project: Sensor Data Display

Project Objective

Create a program that reads data from a simulated temperature and humidity sensor and displays the values in a formatted manner using print statements.

Project Code

```python
import time

# Simulated function to read sensor data
def read_sensor():
    temperature = 25  # Replace with actual sensor reading
    humidity = 60     # Replace with actual sensor reading
    return temperature, humidity

# Main loop to read and display sensor data
while True:
    temp, hum = read_sensor()

    # Display sensor data with formatted print statements
    print(f"Temperature: {temp}°C\tHumidity: {hum}%")
    time.sleep(1)  # Delay to simulate sensor reading intervals
```

Save and Run

1. Save this code as `main.py` on your STM32 NUCLEO.
2. Run the script; the program will display formatted temperature and humidity data in real time.

Check Output

The console will display the temperature and humidity readings every second, formatted with labels and units.

www.ingramcontent.com/pod-product-compliance
Lightning Source LLC
LaVergne TN
LVHW052058060326
832903LV00061B/3427